Stretching Tradition

New Images for Traditional Quilts

Lynn G. Kough

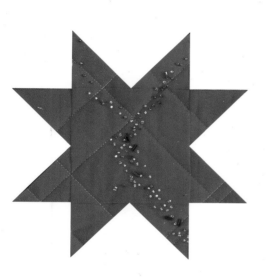

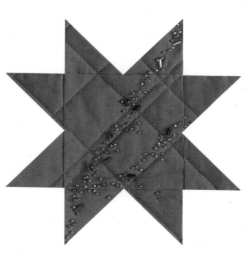

This book belongs to:

Tess Thorsberg

AQS SHOW
PADUCAH, KY
APRIL, 1998

1.50

Editing and production direction by Mary Coyne Penders.
Diagrams and pattern illustrations by Alan C. Kough.
Work Stations developed by the Author.
18 block patterns by Judy Martin.
Book design by Hani Stempler, Character Place, Inc., Atlanta.
Production and project management by Character Place, Inc.,
    Atlanta.
Photography by Sharon Risedorph, San Francisco.
Printing and color separations by Regent Publishing Services,
    Limited, Hong Kong.

First edition.

Library of Congress Cataloging-in-Publication Data

Kough, Lynn G., 1946 –
    Stretching Tradition: New Images for Traditional Quilts

    1. Quilting – Designs   2. Quilting – Techniques   3. Crafts and Hobbies

ISBN 1-881588-13-0

Quilt House Publishing
95 Mayhill Street
Saddle Brook, NJ 07663

 # Dedication

To A.C.K.
Now and forever, amen.

 # Acknowledgements

My unending thanks:

To my husband, Al, for his constant support and countless hours at the computer keyboard.

To Mary Coyne Penders, for her faith in me, her encouragement, her clarity of vision, and her willingness to take a chance on an unknown.

To my terrific students, who took the plunge — creating new and wonderful quilts as they leapt — and taught me as well.

To my good friends, who believed and pushed me to share this idea, especially Barbara, Barbara, Pat, Mary and Joy.

To my Mom, for tying up hundreds of loose ends and turning miles of binding.

Lastly to Nancy, for cheerfully coping with the mess in our hotel room!

Table of Contents

Possibilities, Potential, and Limits

My favorite question is *"What if...?"* That probably explains a great deal.

Do you remember those standardized tests with their section of printed diagrams? We were supposed to imagine the finished shape of the object once the diagram was folded. I always thought that part was fun! *What if...?*

Years later, I tried the geometry teacher's patience by insisting that there was more than one way to proof a problem. To his credit, he allowed me to explore different ways of traveling from beginning to end, even if they weren't the most obvious or direct routes. *What if...?*

After sampling many forms of needlework, quiltmaking seems to be my final destination. Those geometric block patterns are waiting for me, filled with possibilities. There seems to be no end to the ways that I can push or stretch or compress those patterns into something entirely different. *What if...?*

However, with experience came the realization that, for me, unbridled possibilities meant too many decisions and a lack of control in the finished product. Hence the gradual formation of limits in the design process. These limits challenge me to make a cohesive whole in spite of, or because of them. Contradictory perhaps, but limitations can indeed be freeing. It becomes interesting to say, "What if you can *only* do this or that?"

The system you are about to meet literally took form and shape on the floor of a hotel room in Chicago. I cut out the pieces on the dresser top and, as there was no design wall, carefully arranged them on the floor. Then I climbed on and off the bed and a chair trying to get a perspective on just how the colors were working. This methodology also required large cautionary notes to the housekeeping staff about vacuuming!

Since then, happily, my students have been willing to try my ideas and use them to create wonderful quilts. Many of them are reaching far beyond what they had ever attempted previously, and, best of all, they are enjoying themselves!

Here are some of their reactions:

> *"I like that the design is rooted in traditional quiltmaking and that I can then move into a very individual expression of color and space."*

> *"I like the flexibility within a structured framework."*

> *"I can't believe how different the final product is from the original block."*

> *"I'll probably never make another quilt without at least thinking about this system."*

And my favorite —
> *"This is probably the most frustrating, exasperating, exciting, and creative class I have ever taken!"*

Now it's your turn to ask ***"What if...?"*** The following design process, to the best of my knowledge, is my own – though given how many truly "new" ideas there are in this world, it would not surprise me to find someone else somewhere doing similar things. Hope they're having as much fun as I am! I invite you to explore my method, a different path from beginning to end, using a traditional pieced block pattern as your guide. You, too, can indulge in exasperation and creativity! This is going to be fun.

Enjoy the journey!

 # Beginnings

Every journey has to begin somewhere. True enough. The first step is often the most difficult. Also true. Defining a starting point for your quilt will be a great help as you begin. Try using one of these questions as motivation:

- Is there a block pattern you find particularly intriguing?
- Do you own a specific fabric which is begging to be featured?
- Could you celebrate an event or explore a theme?
- How about working with a particular color?
- Do you know of a place or building which evokes a geometric pattern?
- Has a photo, painting, or poster stimulated your creative "juices"?
- Would you like to explore a mood or emotion through color and line?

Or are there so many possibilities that today would be a good day to just reach into the fabric pile and start with whatever appears in your hand?

The most important thing is to choose something — anything! — and get started. It may not be the very best choice of all time, but that really doesn't matter. The worst that can happen is that you will choose to begin again.

Hydroponics by Lynn G. Kough, Middletown, New Jersey. 33″ x 36″.

The Departure

THE DESIGN SYSTEM

At the risk of overworking our metaphor here, I encourage you to follow the map I am providing for your design journey. There will be many opportunities to step off the path and explore on your own—in fact, I encourage that—but for now, proceeding through Parts I and II one step at a time will make all of your forays more fun! Ready? Here we go...

DEFINING THE TERMS

Traditional pieced block patterns in regular, ordinary sizes which anyone can handle or draw for themselves are the basis for this design system. The blocks themselves and the design units taken from them are defined in this system as *sizings, split-outs*, and *splices*. How about that? An entire process requiring only three terms!

Sizings **are full blocks constructed just as the original pattern appears; however, they are made in different finished sizes all in the same quilt.** For example, the design for **Hydroponics** *(p. 9)* uses a Gentleman's Fancy block in fifteen-inch, twelve-inch, nine-inch, and six-inch finished sizes *(Figure 1.1, next page).*

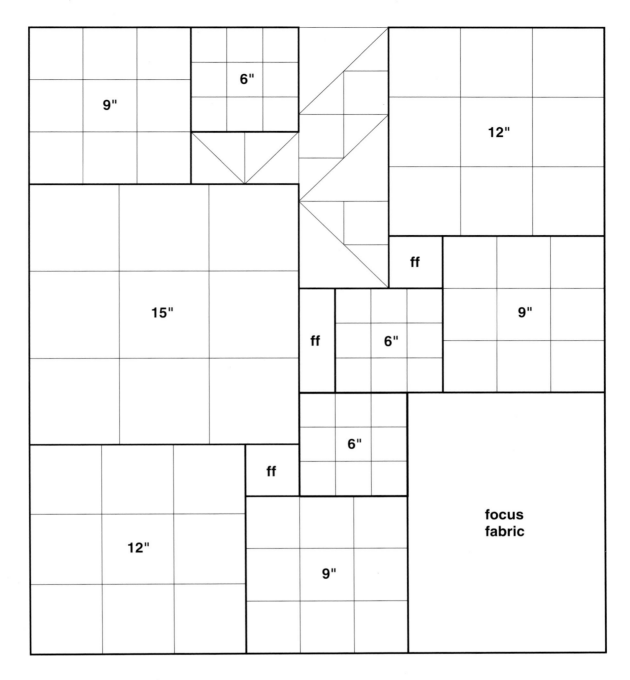

Figure 1.1: *Hydroponics*

***Split-outs* are those units of the block which can be used as separate, complete entities by themselves. They are shapes which are repeated or grouped together in the original block design.** Again looking at a Gentleman's Fancy block, there are three major units which can function as split-outs *(Figure 1.2, p. 12)*. Split-outs are a valuable part of the total design, so it is important to select a block pattern with three or more different units.

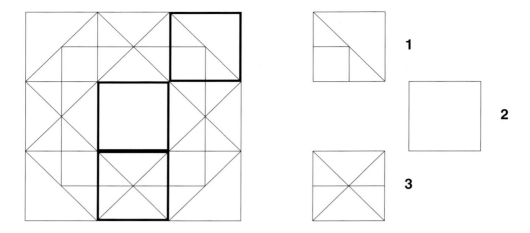

Figure 1.2: *Gentleman's Fancy* - 3 major split-outs

***Splices* occur when blocks are overlapped along design lines or along the grid lines on which the pattern is based.** Usually the blocks are all of one size. The Star and Domino blocks in **Stardust** have been spliced and overlapped *(Figure 1.3).* The quilt is on page 13.

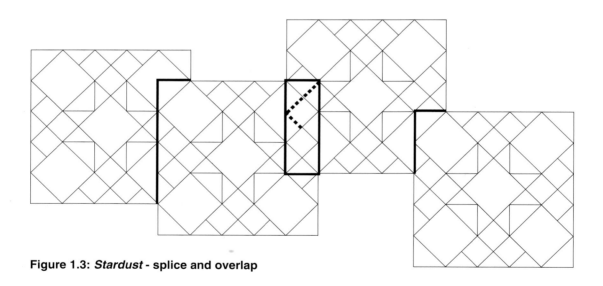

Figure 1.3: *Stardust* - splice and overlap

That's it! These three concepts are the basis for creating new images from traditional blocks, and making your original quilt design as simple or complex as you wish. Most of the quilts based on this method use two of the three parts: **sizings** and **split-outs** *or* **splices** and **split-outs** (because my students found that to be quite enough creativity, thank you very much!). In reality, this system is intended to limit possibilities in order to encourage clarity and focus. Split-outs are always used to *support* the sized or spliced blocks. At any rate, you can certainly take the plunge and use this system in a manner that best suits your motivation and design.

Stardust by Lynn G. Kough, Middletown, New Jersey, 50" x 34".

SELECTING THE BLOCK

Traditional geometric block designs are drawn on a grid. The grid is created from a regular division of the total block area *(Figure 1.4)*.

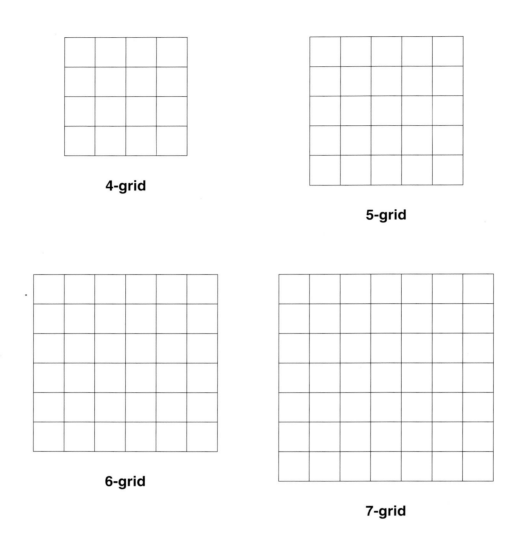

4-grid

5-grid

6-grid

7-grid

Figure 1.4: *Regular block division = grid*

This grid — or framework — provides the beginning and ending points for the lines which form the block's design *(Figures 1.5A & B, p. 15)*. Block designs which are based on a four-, five-, six-, or seven-grid generally work well in this system.

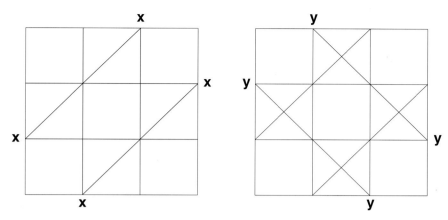

Figure 1.5A: *Connect points on the grid to form design lines*

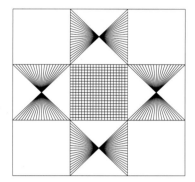

Figure 1.5B: *Block pattern*

When you are selecting a block pattern for the foundation of your quilt design, keep in mind that some blocks will work better than others. Here are some ideas to help you select a workable block.

1. Choose a block which has interesting units, avoiding too many or too few *(Figure 1.6, p. 16)*.
2. Limit open areas and plain corners *(Figure 1.7, p. 16)*.
3. Look for diagonals *(Figure 1.8, p.16)* and internal shapes, such as stars, small nine-patches, arrows, and "geese" *(Figure 1.9, p. 17)*.
4. Look for a block with a center square if you wish to:
   a. feature a particular fabric.
   b. incorporate a special technique.
   c. include some wonderful embellishments.

As soon as you think you've found a block pattern for your quilt, briefly analyze it in the following ways to see how it fits the system.

1. Think about how it will size larger and smaller.
2. Look for large units and smaller divisions for split-outs.
3. Consider whether it is a good choice for splicing.

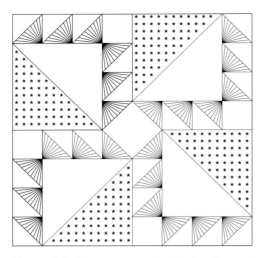

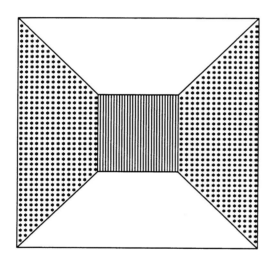

Figure 1.6: *Too many units (L), too few units (R)*

Figure 1.7: *Too open (L), large plain corners (R)*

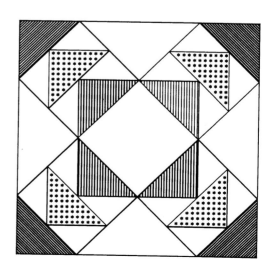

Figure 1.8: *Strong diagonals*

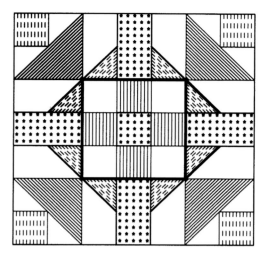

A - *nine patch*
    illusion of square on point

B - *interior star*
    circular illusion

C - arrows

D - "geese"

Figure 1.9: Internal shapes

If the block passes these first criteria, it's time for you to consider it more completely. Get out your pencil and doodling paper, and test the block. Stop at the Work Stations to practice each part of the system as you go along. First use the blocks provided. These are both traditional favorites which you might recognize, and tradition-based designs created by Judy Martin. Then try the block which you have selected.

SIZING

When you think about *sizing* the block (constructing the block in its original pattern in several different finished sizes within one quilt), remember that the object here is to work in measurements which are easy to handle and which free you from relying on printed templates. Anyone can draw these block patterns with a pencil, eraser, *accurate* ruler and graph paper (a *must*). Purchase your graph paper from an art supply store, college bookstore, or quilt shop which carries a reputable brand. This will make your life so much easier.

The complexity of each block design will suggest the best sizings to use. If the block is quite complex, smaller sizes may be difficult to piece; therefore, larger sizes are a better choice. If the block is relatively simple, smaller sizes will enhance the piece and give the illusion of greater complexity.

To determine potential sizes for your block, use the following easy method.

4-Grid Block

Begin with a twelve-inch size if the block is based on a grid of 4. Then add or subtract increments of either 2 or 4 inches to arrive at sizings which will both work well together and be manageable to piece.

BASE SIZE 12 (+ or – 2, 4)		
ADD OR SUBTRACT		**COMPATIBLE BLOCK SIZE GROUPS**
4	=	8, 12, 16, 20 (Fig. 1.10)
2	=	8, 10, 12, 14, 16, 18 (Fig. 1.11)

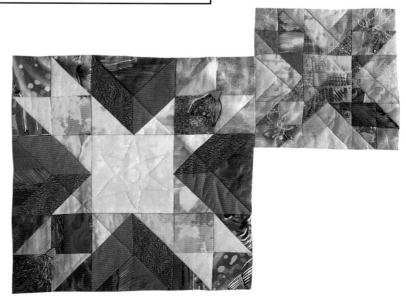

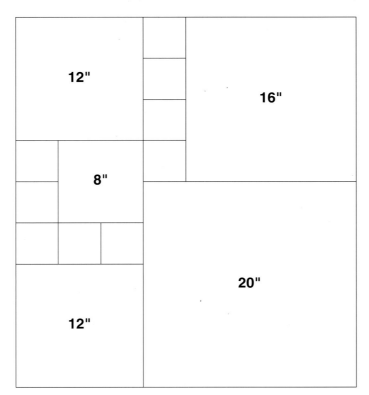

Figure 1.10: *4-grid blocks*

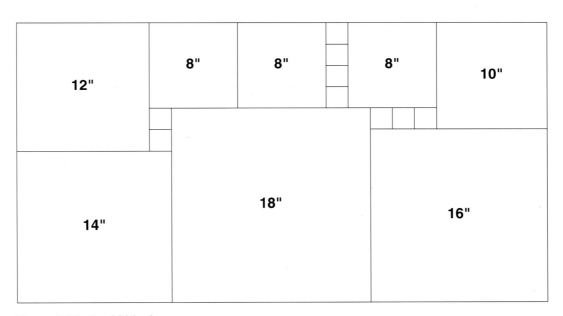

Figure 1.11: *4-grid blocks*

5-Grid Block

Begin with a ten-inch size if the block is based on a grid of five. Then increase and decrease the block in 5″ or 2-1/2″ increments.

BASE SIZE 10 (+ or – 5, 2-1/2)		
ADD OR SUBTRACT		COMPATIBLE BLOCK SIZE GROUPS
5	=	5, 10, 15, 20 (Fig. 1.12)
2-1/2	=	7-1/2, 10, 12-1/2, 15 (Fig. 1.13)

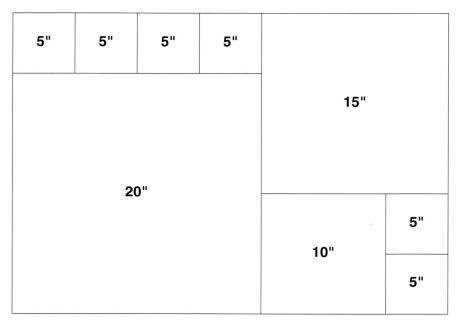

Figure 1.12: *5-grid blocks*

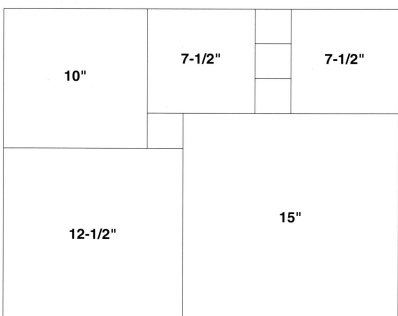

Figure 1.13: *5-grid blocks*

6-Grid Block

Again begin with a twelve-inch size if the block is based on a grid of six. Increase or decrease the block in 3″ or 1-1/2″ increments.

BASE SIZE 12 (+ or − 3, 1-1/2)		
ADD OR SUBTRACT		COMPATIBLE BLOCK SIZE GROUPS
3	=	6, 9, 12, 15 (Fig. 1.14)
1-1/2	=	7-1/2, 9, 10-1/2, 13-1/2 (Fig. 1.15)

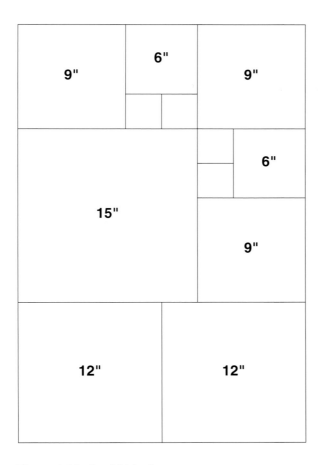

Figure 1.14: *6-grid blocks*

Figure 1.15: *6-grid blocks*

7-Grid Blocks

For a seven grid, begin with a fourteen-inch size. Now increase and decrease the block in 7″ or 3-1/2″ increments.

BASE SIZE 14 (+ or - 7, 3-1/2)		
ADD OR SUBTRACT		COMPATIBLE BLOCK SIZE GROUPS
7	=	7, 14, 21 (Fig. 1.16)
3-1/2	=	10-1/2, 14, 17-1/2 (Fig. 1.17)

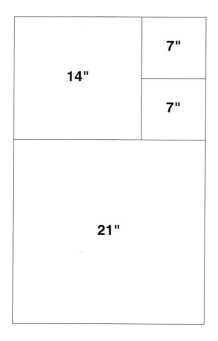

Figure 1.16: *7-grid blocks*

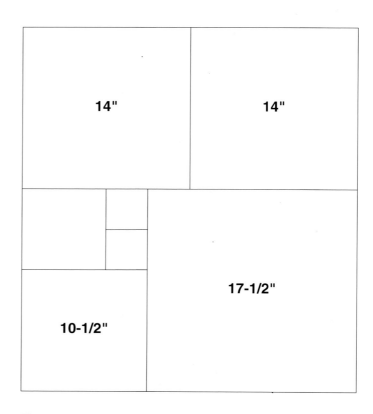

Figure 1.17: *7-grid blocks*

Remember — if the block is complex, larger sizes are a better choice. If the block is relatively simple, smaller sizes will work well.

Use **Work Station I** to practice *sizing blocks of varying grids.*

WORK STATION I - SIZING

Determine the block sizings for each grid (4, 5, 6, 7) based on the method described on pages 18-22. Use 8 to-the-inch graph paper to sketch the blocks given on pages 24 and 25 in several different sizes. Draw outside lines first — simply count each square on the graph paper as one inch.

A sample block has been done for you.

A. Analyze the block to determine and mark the grid. Place tracing paper over the block drawing.

B. Determine the sizings and the measurement of a grid area (size of block divided by grid: 12 ÷ 6 = 2).

C. Draw the block in the various sizes. Use the midpoint on the side of a graph paper square for a 1/2" measurement.

Sample Block

C.

A.

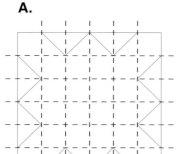

B.

Block size	Grid area =
6"	1"
9"	1-1/2"
12"	2"
15"	2-1/2"

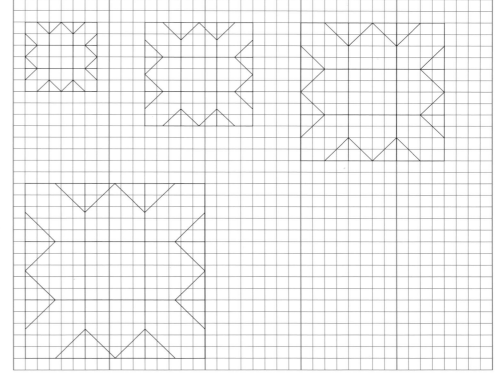

4-Grid Block

A.

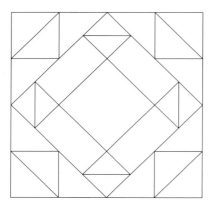 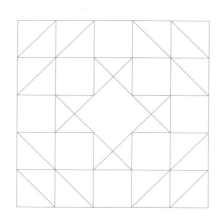

B.

Block size	Grid area =		Block size	Grid area =
(+ or − 4) _____	_____		(+ or − 2) _____	_____
_____	_____		_____	_____
_____	_____		_____	_____
_____	_____		_____	_____
			_____	_____
			_____	_____

5-Grid Block

A.

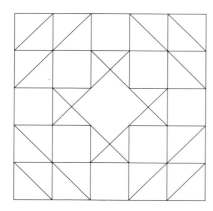

B.

Block size	Grid area =		Block size	Grid area =
(+ or − 5) _____	_____		(+ or − 2-1/2) _____	_____
_____	_____		_____	_____
_____	_____		_____	_____
_____				

6-Grid Block

A.

B.

	Block size	Grid area =		Block size	Grid area =
(+ or − 3)	_____	_____	(+ or − 1-1/2)	_____	_____
	_____	_____		_____	_____
	_____	_____		_____	_____
	_____	_____		_____	_____

7-Grid Block

A.

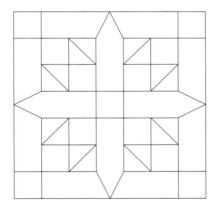 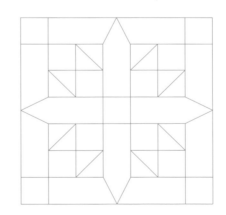

B.

	Block size	Grid area =		Block size	Grid area =
(+ or − 7)	_____	_____	(+ or − 3-1/2)	_____	_____
	_____	_____		_____	_____
	_____	_____		_____	_____

SPLIT-OUTS

Look at the block pattern and its grid to determine how many potential **split-out** units (shapes repeated or grouped together in the block design) it contains. Keep in mind that these units will function in several ways as you plan your design.

The many jobs of split-out units include:

1. filling in spaces between the complete blocks.
2. carrying color movement along the surface of the quilt.
3. extending design lines.
4. creating the background on which larger blocks float.
5. becoming the pieces which carry the theme of the quilt while larger areas fade to equal or lesser importance.

Split-outs are the "glue" which hold the blocks together in a total design. Based on its design lines and its grid, the simple block shown below in *Figures 1.18A & B* contains four large and four smaller split-out units.

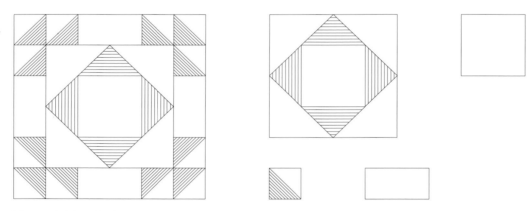

Figure 1.18A: *Split-outs from block*

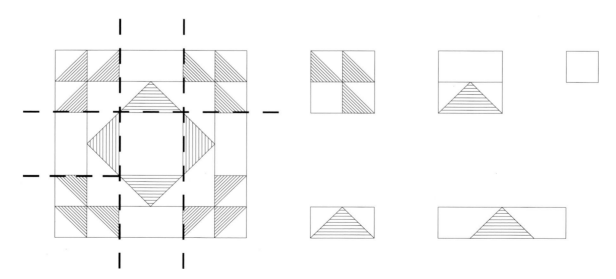

Figure 1.18B: *Split-outs from addition of grid lines*

Use **Work Station II** for practice in *identifying split-out units* within the blocks.

(blocks given on page 28)

WORK STATION II - SPLIT-OUTS

Find as many split-out units as you can in each of the blocks given on page 28. Remember to look for both design lines and grid lines. A sample block has been done for you.

A. Place a sheet of tracing paper over the blocks. For each block, first trace over split-out areas based on design lines.

B. Move the tracing paper, placing a clean space over the block. Now add grid lines to the block.

C. Trace over any additional split-out units.

Sample Block

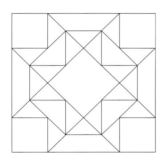

split-out from design lines

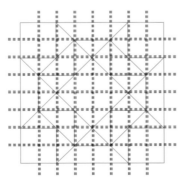

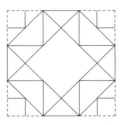

split-outs with addition of grid lines

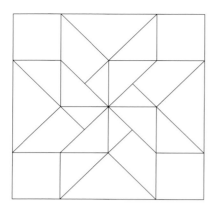

4-grid

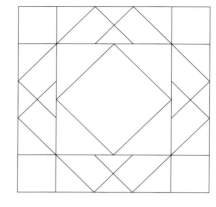

5-grid

6-grid

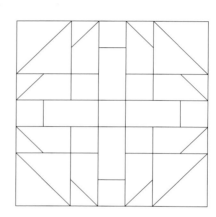

7-grid

SPLICING

Decide whether your block pattern is a good candidate for ***splicing*** (overlapping blocks along design lines or grid lines). Splicing can be used to:

1. create transparency within the blocks.
2. make portions of the blocks disappear.
3. create new shapes as the blocks move together.

It is fairly simple to slide part of one block under another, but can it be done so that the resulting shapes are interesting, rather than repetitive, downright ugly, or impossible to piece?

First draw two identical blocks, one on plain or graph paper and the second on tracing paper. This allows you to see the second block overlapping the first. Test them in the following ways:

1. Overlap the bottom right corner and the top left corner of the two blocks *(Figure 1.19A)*. Can they share a common corner?
2. Overlap the right side of one block with the left side of the other block *(Figure 1.19B)*. Are the design lines compatible? Are new design lines formed which enhance the original pattern? Also test the blocks by overlapping top and bottom sides.
3. Move the overlapping block up or down, matching grid lines or design areas *(Figure 1.19C)*. Is the block suitable for a partial splice?
4. Again overlap the blocks, this time using half of each side *(Figure 1.19D)*. Does this create interesting new shapes? Are the design lines working together cohesively?

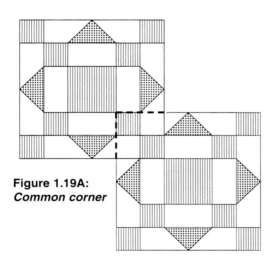

Figure 1.19A:
Common corner

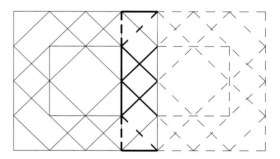

Figure 1.19B: *Full side splice*

Figure 1.19D: *Half side splice*

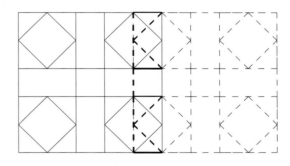

Figure 1.19C: *Partial splice (full side stepped)*

5. Move the overlapping block up or down, once again matching grid lines or design areas *(Figure 1.19E)*. Does this block lend itself to a partial splice?

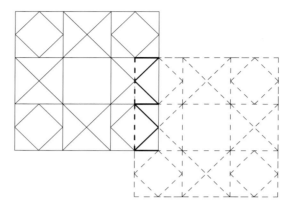

Figure 1.19E: *Partial splice (half side stepped)*

Although each of these steps is shown with a different block, you should test your block in all five ways. If none of the results please you, try another block pattern.

Many blocks are not suitable for splicing. *Figure 1.20* will easily convince you of this. Don't be fainthearted. You will find one or more blocks with great potential for your special quilt.

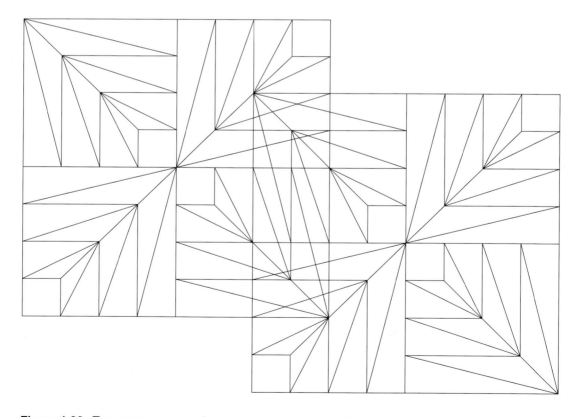

Figure 1.20: *Too many narrow pieces, not suitable for splicing*

Use **Work Station III** to practice the five *splicing* tests.

WORK STATION III - SPLICING

Test the blocks given on page 32 for splicing possibilities. A sample block has been done for you.

A. Trace each block onto tracing paper.

B. Move the traced image over the original.

C. Test each type of splice.
    1. common corner
    2. full side splice
    3. partial side splice (full side stepped)
    4. half side splice
    5. half side partial splice (half side stepped)

Sample Block

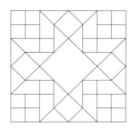

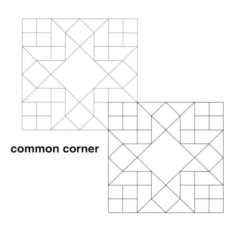

common corner

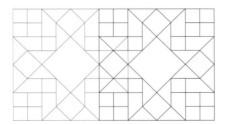

full side splice

half side splice

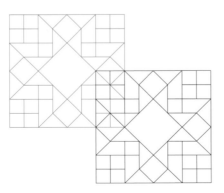

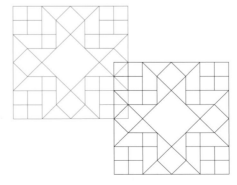

partial side splice
(full side stepped)

half side partial splice
(half side stepped)

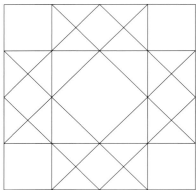

4-grid

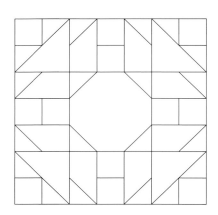

5-grid

6-grid

7-grid

SAMPLE BLOCK ANALYSES

To help you make your final selection, let's examine some sample block patterns and evaluate their suitability for sizing, split-outs, or splicing. As you audition blocks, remember not to lose sight of your original concept. The block pattern should help to carry out your theme or motivation.

Each of the following blocks have been evaluated for sizing or splicing and for split-out units. Suggested block sizes are given and split-out units are delineated.

Four-grid blocks *(Figures 1.21A, B, C)*

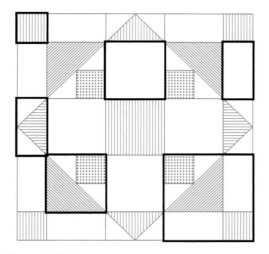

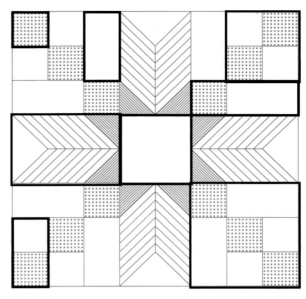

Figure 1.21A:

four-grid block   *6 split-outs*

diagonal movement   *sizing: 8", 12", 16", 20"*

Figure 1.21B:

four-grid block   *8 split-outs*

good corner motion   *sizing: 8", 12", 16", 20"*

internal star

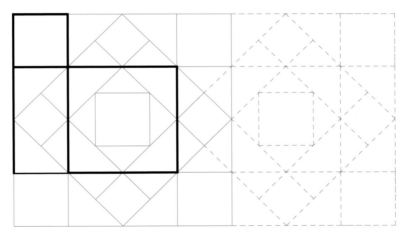

Figure 1.21C: *four-grid block*   *3 split-outs*

full side splice   *12"*

Five-grid blocks *(Figures 1.22A, B, C)*

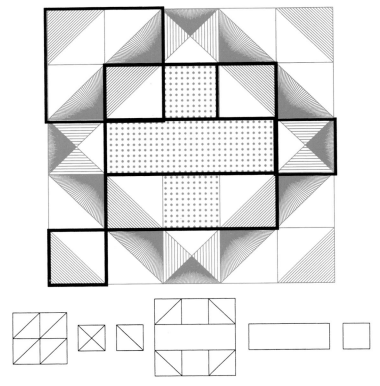

Figure 1.22A: *five-grid block*   *6 split-outs*

diagonals   *sizing: 7-1/2″, 10″, 17-1/2″*

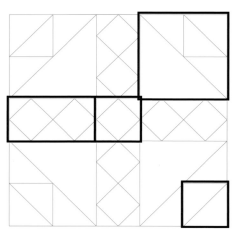

Figure 1.22B: *five-grid block*

4 split-outs

good opposing movement

sizing: 10″, 12-1/2″, 15″

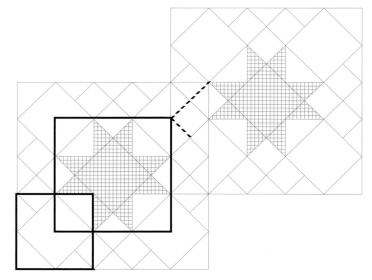

Figure 1.22C: *five-grid block*   *2 split-outs based on grid*

full side stepped   *10″*

new design lines

Six-grid blocks *(Figures 1.23A, B, C)*

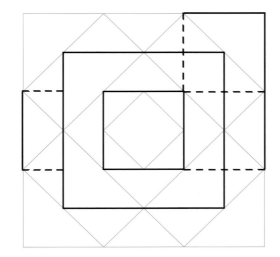

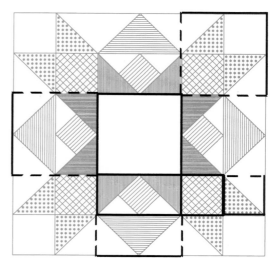

Figure 1.23B:

six-grid block   *7 split-outs*

internal star   *sizing: 9″, 12″, 15″, 18″*

Figure 1.23A: *six-grid block*   *5 split-outs*

strong diagonals   *sizing: 9″, 12″, 15″*

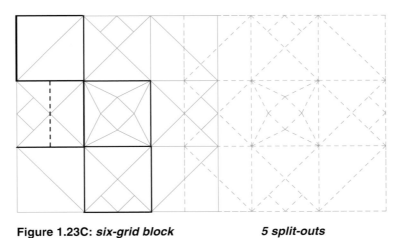

Figure 1.23C: *six-grid block*   *5 split-outs*

spliced half side   *12″*

new design lines

Seven-grid blocks *(Figures 1.24A, B, C)*

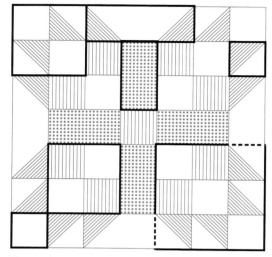

Figure 1.24A: *seven-grid block*
7 split-outs
sizing: 14", 17-1/2"

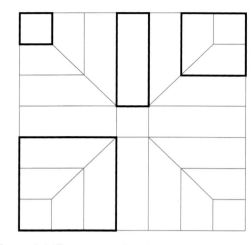

Figure 1.24B: *seven-grid block*
4 split-outs
sizing: 10-1/2", 14"

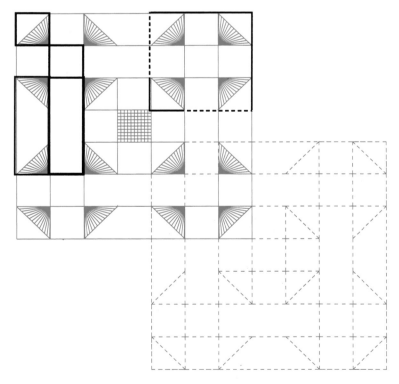

Figure 1.24C: *seven grid block*   *5 split-outs*
common corner splice   *14˝*

Now you are well into your journey, becoming more creative with each step. You understand the terminology, you've analyzed and selected a block pattern, and you're eager to move on. Good! ***What if...?***

Autumn Sun by Patricia D. Ryan, Clarksburg, New Jersey, 50" x 37".

October by Lucy H. Minder, Oceanport, New Jersey. 44" x 58-1/2".

DESIGN STRATEGY

All designers have tools which help them as they work. The supplies needed for mapping your quilt design are as follows:

- graph paper (8 or 10 squares to-the-inch)
- #2 pencils
- a sturdy eraser
- fine-point black permanent marker
- tracing paper
- colored pencils
- your sense of adventure!!

VISUAL WEIGHT AND MOVEMENT

Before taking pencil in hand, let's briefly consider the ideas of visual weight and visual movement. When we look at a quilt, we first see the impact of the design as a whole and then we see the details. Our eyes travel around the design, taking in shapes and colors, noticing some areas more than others. Shape, size, and color affect visual weight.

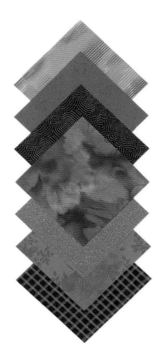

1. Larger shapes might appear heavier.
2. Darker shades seem heavier than lighter ones.
3. Bright, vibrant colors are more dense than soft pastels.

The placement of shapes and colors in the design controls the viewer's initial impression, and then determines where the eye moves over and around the surface of the quilt. Since most of us read from left to right and top to bottom of a page, this influences our perceptions. *We tend to see designs from top left to bottom right.* Certainly this is worth consideration when formulating a design, but it's not the only way to go.

Perhaps this reading pattern explains the appeal of a strong diagonal pattern. Diagonals achieved through the use of shapes and colors always make a dynamic, visually interesting quilt. Patti Ryan created bright sunlight across her quilt, **Autumn Sun** *(p. 37)*, by placing the lightest values of fabrics on the diagonal and carrying that line into the borders. Conversely, the strong v-shape in Lucy Minder's quilt, **October** *(p. 38)*, is created by the placement of the darker fabric values. Think how enjoyable it is to see an Irish Chain, Jacob's Ladder, Mariner's Compass, or blocks set on point. All of these use diagonal motion in the design.

After you create the framework for your quilt design, color and fabric will bring it to life. **Remember** these two important hints as you face that empty graph paper:

1. Keep the design simple.
2. Incorporate some kind of diagonal motion.

PLANNING FOR SIZINGS

You need not include all compatible sizings of your block in one design. A minimum of three is a good general rule. Working on 8 squares to-the-inch or 10 squares to-the-inch graph paper allows you to map out the entire design on one sheet. I find that helpful.

For an example, let's work with my favorite sizes — 6″, 9″, 12″, and 15″, using a 6-grid block —Gentleman's Fancy.

Step 1: Placement of the largest blocks — 15″

    A. Determine an outside measurement for the quilt and designate a top side. To arrive at a workable size, choose one of these methods:
- Add together the size of two large blocks [15 + 15 = 30]
    or
- Add together the sizes of three different blocks
[15 + 12 + 9 = 36]

When you are working with a square, use the resulting number from either method 1 or 2 as the dimension of all sides. Based on the sample blocks, you could choose to begin with an outside measurement of either 30″ square or 36″ square.

When you are working with a rectangle, use the total number from method 1 for two sides, and the total number from method 2 for the opposite two sides. These sample numbers yield a rectangle 30″ x 36″.

You may wish to adjust these measurements as you proceed, but this is a good starting point.

    B. Decide where to place the 15″ block. Draw the outside lines of the block on your graph paper. The example shows three placement options *(Figures 2.1A, B, C, p. 41)*.

Placing the largest block

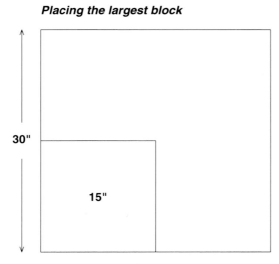

Figure 2.1A: *Step 1, option 1*

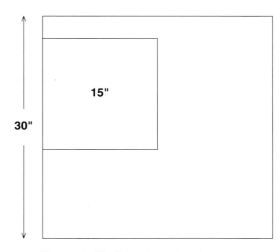

Figure 2.1B: *Step 1, option 2*

Figure 2.1C: *Step 1, option 3*

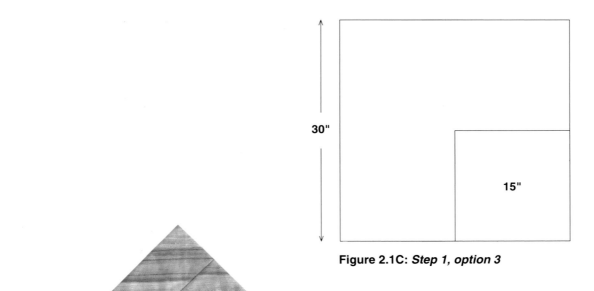

Step 2: Placement of the second largest size — 12″

    A. Add two of this block size.

    B. Draw the outside lines of the blocks. The example shows three placement options *(Figures 2.2A, B, C)*. **Remember**, the full blocks do not have to fill the entire design area by themselves. The split-outs will complete your framework.

Placing the second largest block

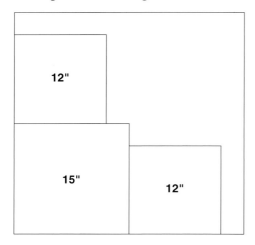

Figure 2.2A: *Step 2, option 1*

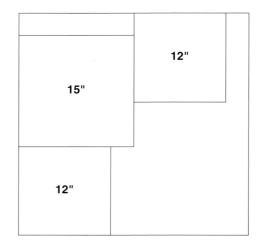

Figure 2.2B: *Step 2, option 2*

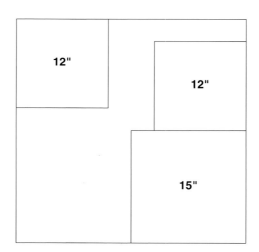

Figure 2.2C: *Step 2, option 3*

Step 3: Placement of the next smaller size — 9″

    A. Add two or three of this block size.

    B. Placement choices are more limited as open areas in the design space become smaller *(Figures 2.3A, B, C)*. You may decide to change your outside measurements at this point to better accommodate the blocks.

Placing the next smaller block

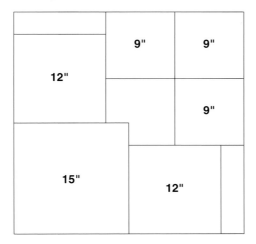

Figure 2.3A: *Step 3, option 1*

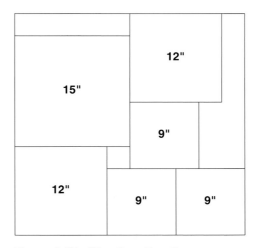

Figure 2.3B: *Step 3, option 2*

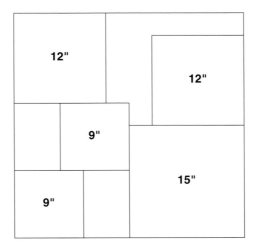

Figure 2.3C: *Step 3, option 3*

Step 4: Placement of smallest complete blocks — 6″
(Don't confuse these with a large split-out.)

    A. This step is optional. Your block design may not lend itself to anything this small.

    B. If you use these smallest blocks, work one to four into your design *(Figures 2.4A, B, C)*. The smaller blocks really add sparkle.

Placing the smallest block

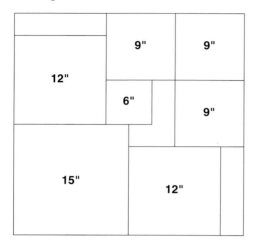

Figure 2.4A: *Step 4, option 1*

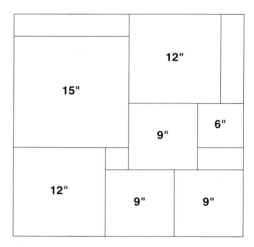

Figure 2.4B: *Step 4, option 2*

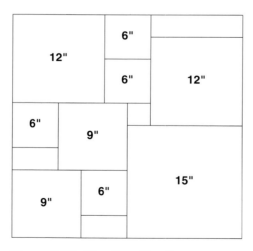

Figure 2.4C: *Step 3, option 3*

Note: As you add each block size, you may find that you need to move, add, or eliminate something from a previous step. At times everything falls easily into place; at other times you'll need several revisions. The key is to have fun trying different possibilities and be open to seeing what your design is "telling" you.

Step 5: Addition of split-outs

    A. The split-outs hold together all of the different sized blocks. Their placement makes everything work as a cohesive unit. To adequately see this, you need to have the design lines show in the full blocks.

    B. Add the design lines into your blocks *(Figures 2.5A, B, C)*.

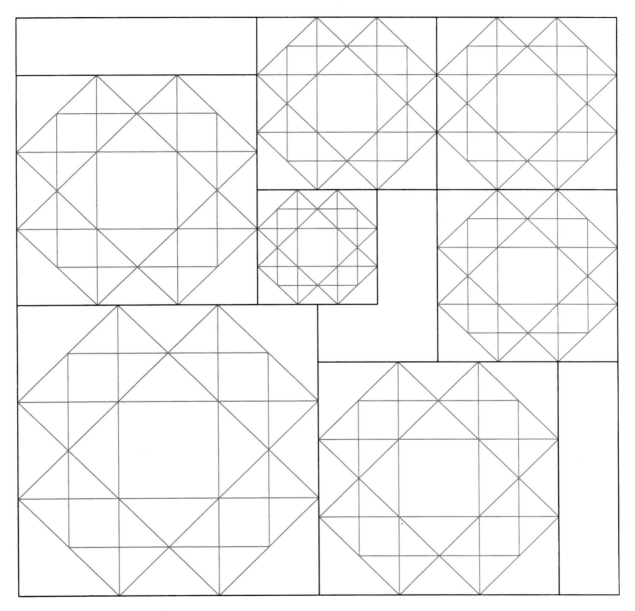

Figure 2.5A: *Step 5B, option 1*
        Filling in the design lines

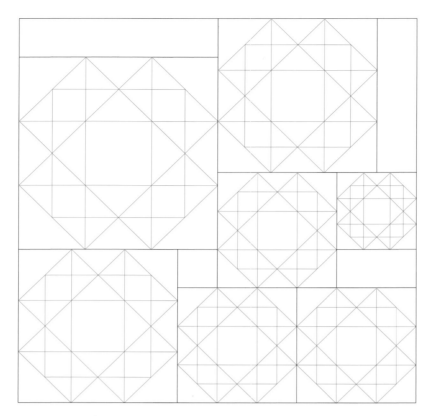

Figure 2.5B: *Step 5B, option 2*

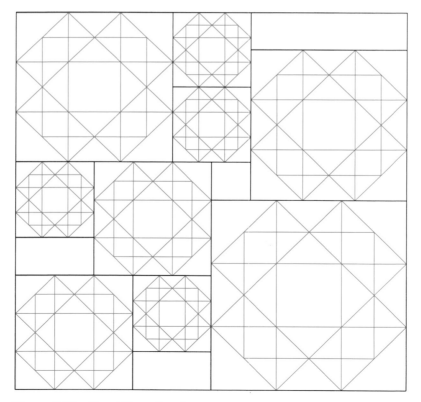

Figure 2.5C: *Step 5B, option 3*

C. Look at the split-outs available from the block. In the example, split-outs are squares of 5″, 4″, 3″, and 2″ *(Figure 2.6)*. Three split-out designs will be used to carry the design lines from one block to another throughout the whole quilt *(Figure 2.7)*.

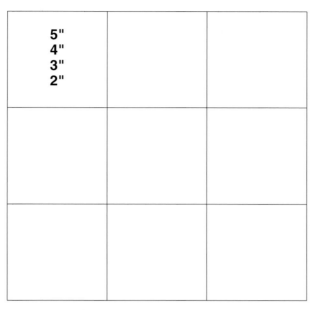

5"
4"
3"
2"

Figure 2.6: *15" block = 5" split-out*

12" block = 4" split-out

9" block = 3" split-out

6" block = 2" split-out

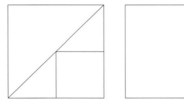 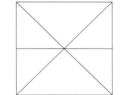

Figure 2.7: *Split-outs to be added*

D. Add the split-outs *(Figures 2.8A, B, C)*.

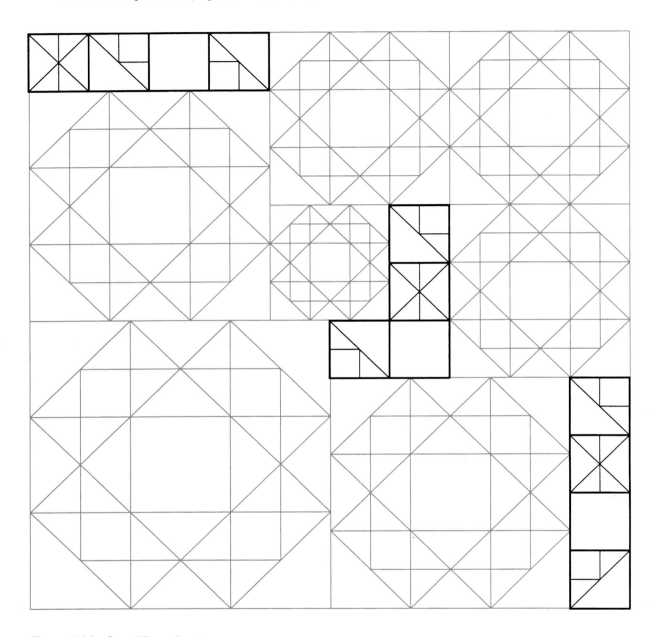

Figure 2.8A: *Step 5D, option 1*
Adding split-outs

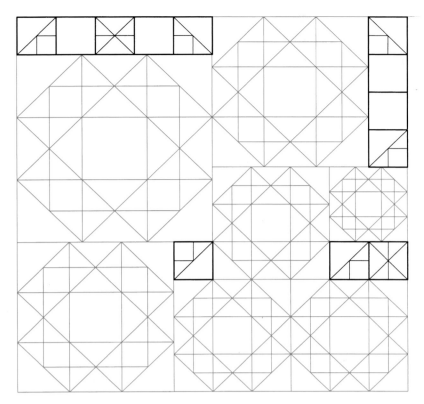

Figure 2.8B: *Step 5D, option 2*

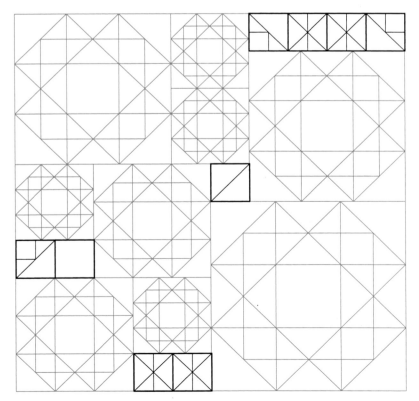

Figure 2.8C: *Step 5D, option 3*

Remember the second way to create the split-outs you need — imaginary lines. Look at the design grid of your block (the regular division of the total block area). The grid line may be missing from the final block design, but if you need a piece which would include it —why not? Go ahead and use the grid line to create the split-out unit *(Figures 2.9A, B*; also refer to *Figure 1.18, p. 26).*

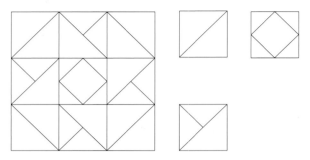

Figure 2.9A: *Split-outs from block*

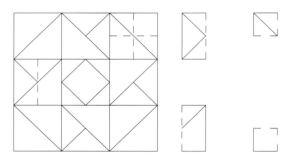

Figure 2.9B: *Split-outs from addition of grid lines*

Occasionally there are one or two spaces where a split-out won't fit. You may simply need to fill this space with a single piece of fabric. If there are a fair number of these, however, your design probably needs to be rearranged. With compatible block sizes, most everything fits together. Try re-working the puzzle to get a better design if this is not happening for you.

Now let's try designing another quilt, this time using a 5-grid block. The available sizings are 7-1/2˝, 10˝, 12-1/2˝, and 15˝. The half-inch sizes are drawn on the graph paper halfway through a full block *(Figure 2.10).*

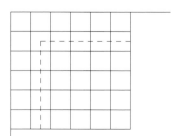

Figure 2.10: *Drawing half-inch measurements*

Follow these steps:

Step 1: Determine the outside measurement; place the largest block.

Step 2: Add two or three of the next smaller size.

Step 3: Add two or three of the third size.

Step 4: [*optional*] Add the smallest size as needed. If there seem to be too many of these, go back and rearrange steps 1, 2, and 3.

Step 5: The available split-outs for these block sizes are 1-1/2″, 2″, 2-1/2″, and 3″. Fill in the design lines of the full blocks. Add the split-outs, choosing those which carry along the lines of the larger blocks.

Here are some possible results of this exercise *(Figures 2.11A, B)*.

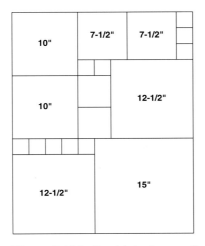

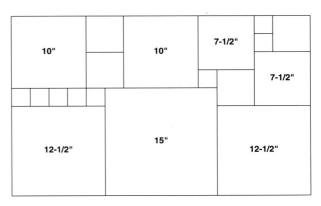

Figure 2.11B: *5-grid design, option 2*

Figure 2.11A: *5-grid design, option 1*

As strange as it may sound, be open to serendipity as you create your quilt. Many of these quilts seem to design themselves. Often you can just let the design happen. You will start to draw in the larger blocks and the split-out shapes will fall into place as if by magic. I don't know about you, but I firmly believe that quilts will "tell" you how they wish to be designed. Enjoy listening!

Use **Work Station IV** to practice creating *sizing layouts.*

WORK STATION IV - SIZING LAYOUT

Practice creating sizing layouts for blocks of each grid size. Draw on your 8 to-the-inch graph paper. Remember to follow these steps.
1. Determine the compatible block sizings.
2. Figure an outside measurement.
3. Draw the split-out units. (Did you add grid lines to create additional split-outs?)

4. Draw the outside lines for one or two of the largest blocks.
5. Add two or three of the next smaller size.
6. Add one, two, or three of the third size.
7. Add the smallest size as needed.
8. Fill in the split-out units.

4-Grid

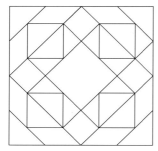

1. _____ or _____
_____ _____
_____ _____
_____ _____
_____
_____

2. _____ x _____
or _____ x _____

5-Grid

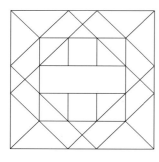

1. _____ or _____
_____ _____
_____ _____
_____ _____
_____

2. _____ x _____
or _____ x _____

6-Grid

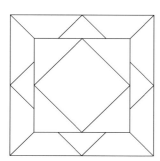

1. _____ or _____
_____ _____
_____ _____
_____

2. _____ x _____
or _____ x _____

7-Grid

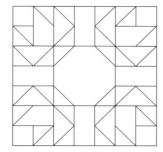

1. ——— or ———
———   ———
———   ———

2. ——— x ———
or ——— x ———

PLANNING FOR SPLICING

A design framework created from splices and split-outs uses blocks all of one size. Look at the following four ways to splice blocks together *(Figure 2.12).*

- common corner
- full side
- half side
- half side stepped

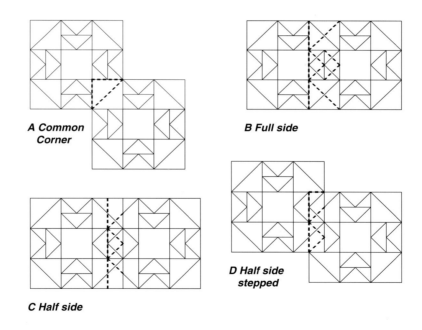

A Common Corner

B Full side

C Half side

D Half side stepped

Figure 2.12: *Four splices*

As a first example, let's work through using a 12″ T-block and splicing some common corners.

Step 1: Draw the outside area of the blocks and the corners which they share *(Figure 2.13)*.

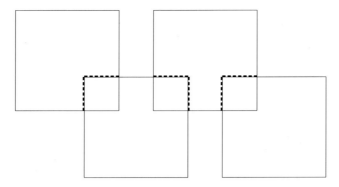

Figure 2.13: *Step 1 - Splice common corners*

Step 2: Once you have this in place, you can draw an outside perimeter to your design *(Figure 2.14)*.

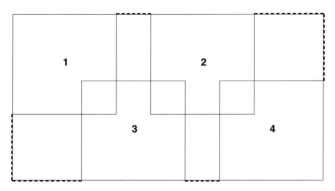

Figure 2.14: *Step 2 - Add outside perimeter*

Step 3: Add the design lines to the blocks *(Figure 2.15A)*.

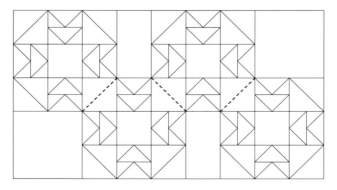

Figure 2.15A: *Step 3 - Add design lines*

Step 4: Determine which split-outs will fill the open spaces and enhance the design lines of the spliced blocks *(Figure 2.15B)*.

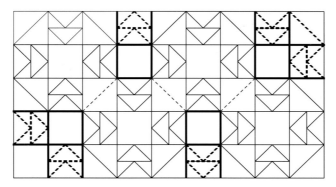

Figure 2.15B: *Step 4 - Add split-outs*

Now try a 12″ block using full side splices. The sample block is called *Around the Corner (Figure 2.16)*.

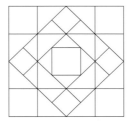

Figure 2.16: *Block design*

Step 1: Draw three blocks, splicing the right side of block one to the left side of block two, and the left side of block three to the right side of block two. *(Figure 2.17)*.

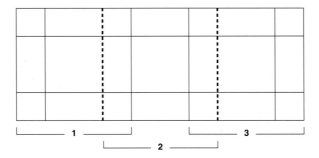

Figure 2.17: *Step 1 - Full side splices*

Step 2: Draw block four beneath block one, splicing the top of block four to the bottom of block one *(Figure 2.18)*.

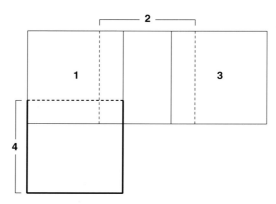

Figure 2.18: *Step 2 - Full side splice, top to bottom*

Step 3: Draw a full block to the right of block four, beneath blocks two and three *(Figure 2.19)*.

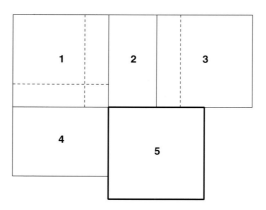

Figure 2.19: *Step 3 - Add a complete block*

Step 4: Draw the outside perimeter to complete a rectangle 24″ x 30″ and fill in the block design lines *(Figure 2.20)*.

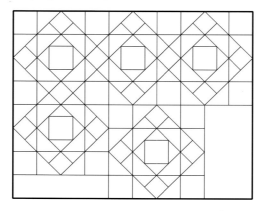

Figure 2.20: *Step 4 - Add outside perimeter and block design lines*

Step 5: Choose split-outs to fill the open areas. The example uses two 3″ squares, one 3″ x 6″ rectangle, and two 6″ squares *(Figure 2.21)*.

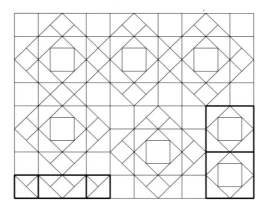

Figure 2.21: *Step 5 - Add split-out units*

You can design a wonderful quilt using just one splicing technique or you may wish to incorporate several *(Figures 2.22A, B)*. For a really fun challenge, try using four or five splices at least once in a design.

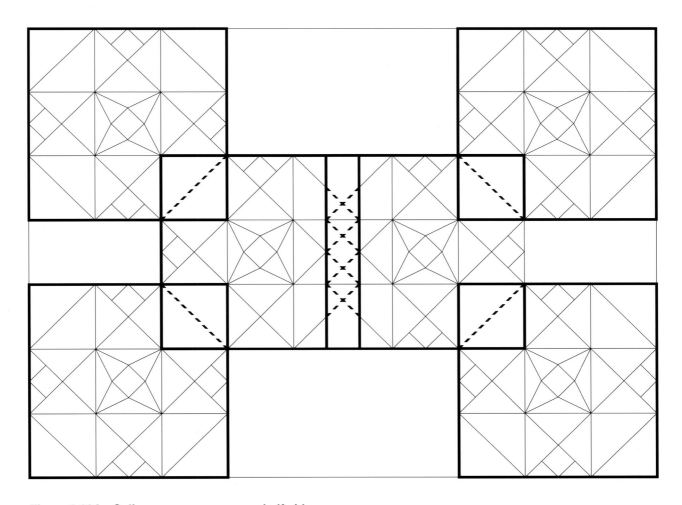

Figure 2.22A: *Splices - common corner, half side*

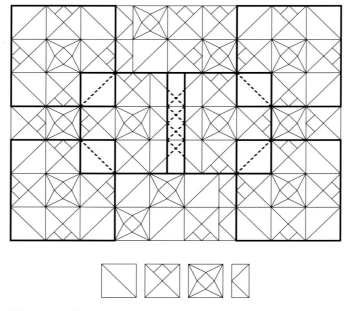

Figure 2.22B: *Addition of split-out units*

Here's one made with T-blocks *(Figure 2.23)*. Four different splices are incorporated into **Starfire** *(p. 59)*.

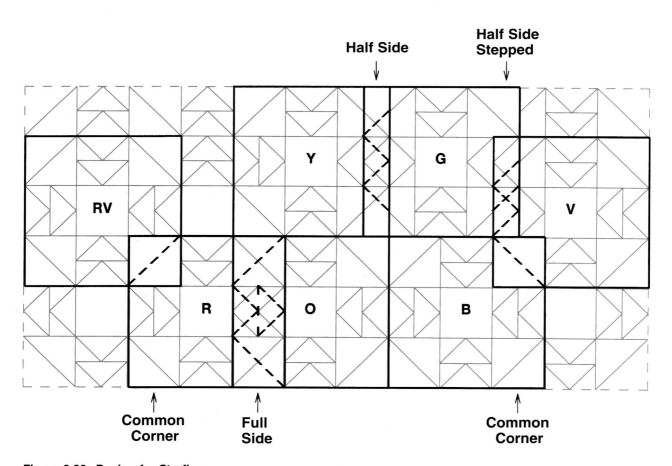

Figure 2.23: *Design for Starfire*

Starfire by Lynn G. Kough, Middletown, New Jersey. 36" x 59".

Use **Work Station V** to practice creating *splicing layouts.*

WORK STATION V - SPLICING LAYOUT

Create several spliced layouts for each given block. Choose from the five splices:
- common corner
- full side
- full side stepped
- half side
- half side stepped

Use three blocks, five blocks, or seven blocks in your layout design. Remember that all these blocks are the same size. Draw on your 8 to-the-inch graph paper.

1. Draw the outside edges of spliced blocks.
2. Draw an outside perimeter.
3. Add the design lines to the blocks.
4. Alongside your layout, draw the split-out units from the block.
5. Fill in your layout with split-outs.

4-Grid

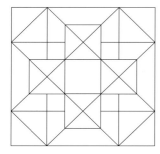

Try several splices.

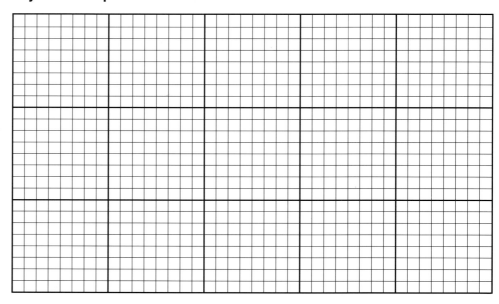

5-Grid

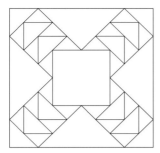

Try several splices.

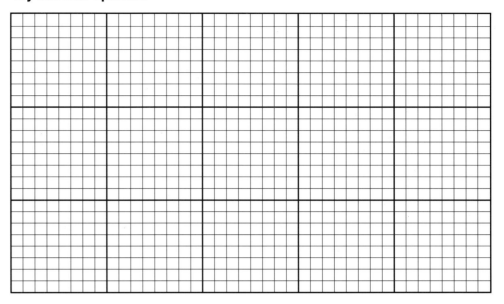

6-Grid

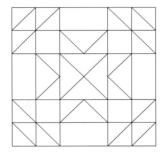

Try several splices.

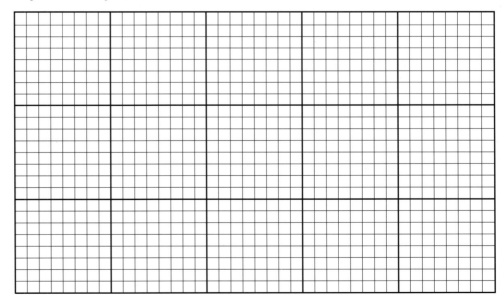

7-Grid

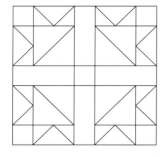

Try several splices.

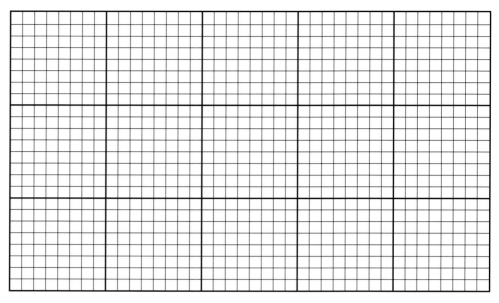

COMBINING SIZINGS, SPLICES AND SPLIT-OUTS

You may wish to dash headlong into this system and use sizings, splices, and split-outs all in one design. Fine! Go for it!!

I would suggest drawing in the spliced blocks first. Then add the sized blocks, from largest to smallest. Last, fill in and "glue" everything together with split-outs *(Figures 2.24A, B, C)*.

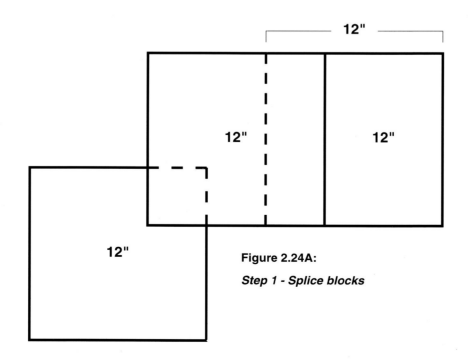

Figure 2.24A:

Step 1 - Splice blocks

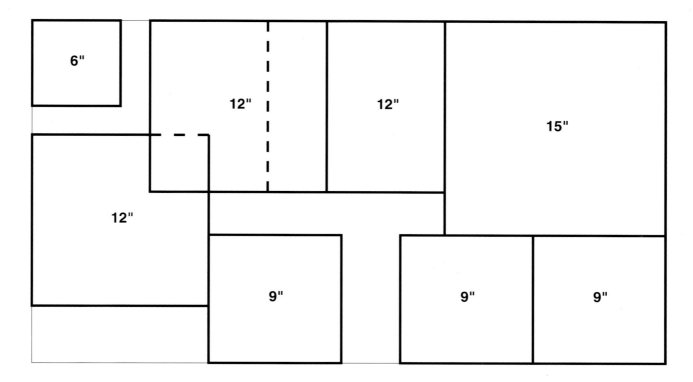

Figure 2.24B: *Step 2 - Add sized blocks and perimeter*

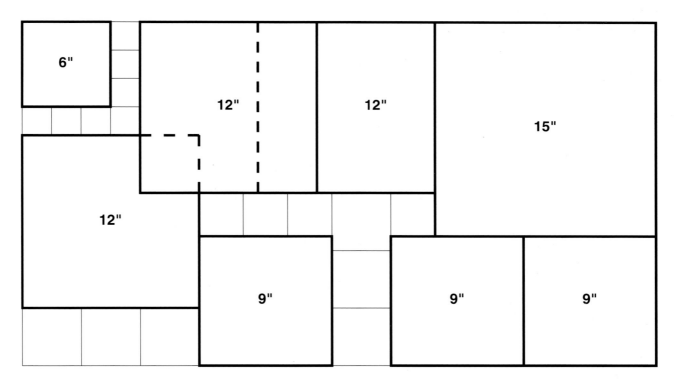

Figure 2.24C: *Sizes, split-outs, and splices combined*

PLANNING THE CONSTRUCTION

Before you settle on a finished design, consider how you will piece the entire quilt top together. Have you created an overwhelming challenge where no two pieces have edges which begin and end in the same line of stitching, or can you see at least some logic to the way the pieces all fit together? Remember the blessing of partial seams (certain seams sewn only part of their length at one stage in the piecing process and completed later in the construction).

Here are suggested methods for piecing the quilt top.

1. Stitch all quilt blocks and split-out units individually. Combine these into larger areas and stitch together. Sew the larger areas together to complete the top *(Figure 2.25, p. 65)*.

2. Stitch together long horizontal units. These will be formed from partial areas of blocks, as well as split-outs *(Figure 2.26A, p. 66)*. Conversely, find long vertical units which can be stitched together. You may have to combine some units into larger areas before stitching the vertical seams *(Figure 2.26B, p. 66)*.

3. Stitch a full block and its surrounding split-outs into a larger unit. Sew the larger units together. *Caution:* Be aware that you may need to sew a portion of one or two full blocks into another unit. Look for the longest complete seams to plan these units *(Figures 2.27A, B, p. 67)*.

If your finished design presents more than a reasonable challenge for sewing together, the solution is simple. Rearrange your blocks and try again. Actually, there are few designs that can't be stitched together somehow. It's really a question of how comfortable you are with the process.

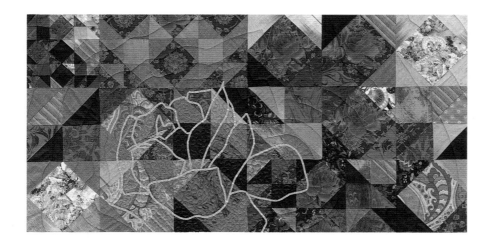

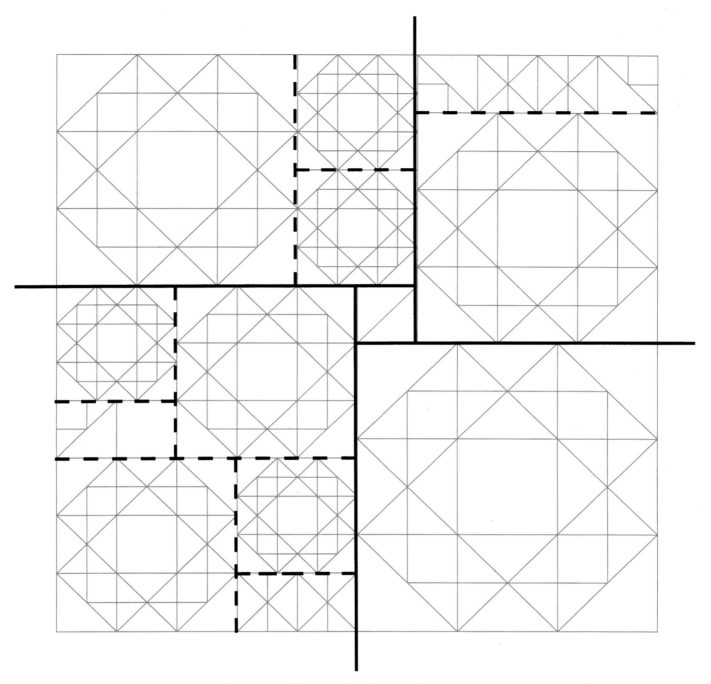

Figure 2.25: 1. *Stitch together each complete block and split-out unit.*

2. **– – – – – – –** *Combine these into larger areas.*

3. ——————— *Sew larger areas together around center split-out unit using a partial seam.*

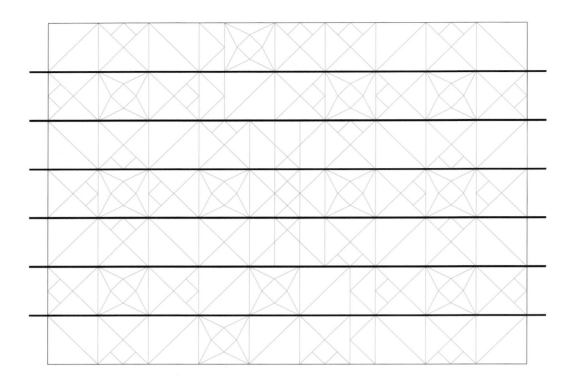

Figure 2.26A: ━━━━━━━ *Stitch long horizontal units together.*

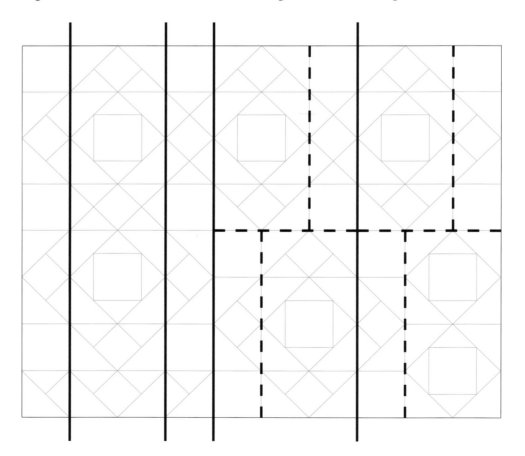

Figure 2.26B: ― ― ― ― ― *Combine small units into larger areas.*

━━━━━━━ *Stitch long vertical units together.*

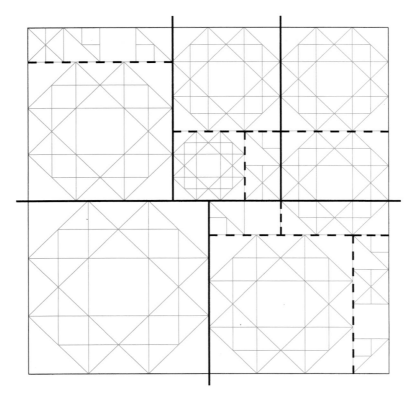

Figure 2.27A: ‐ ‐ ‐ ‐ ‐ ‐ ‐ *Stitch smaller units into larger areas.*

——————— *Stitch large areas together.*

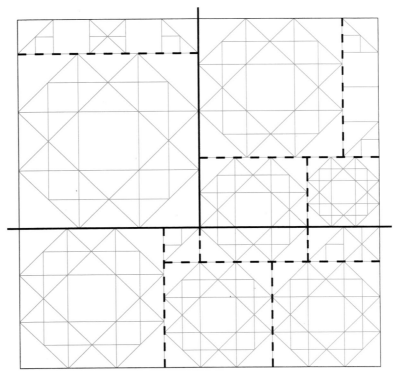

Figure 2.27B: ‐ ‐ ‐ ‐ ‐ ‐ ‐ *Stitch smaller units into larger areas.*

——————— *Stitch large areas together.*

CREATING BORDERS

Borders are one of several milestones on your design journey. Some quilts clearly require them; others are happy without them. What kind of border (if any) will complete your design?

1. *Melded borders* flow in and out of the central portion of the design. They originate in the quilt and move out to complete it. These borders may contain split-outs or portions of blocks which extend into the border area *(Figure 2.28)*. Bea Johnson's **When You Wish Upon a Star** flows beautifully between the central portion of the design and the borders *(p. 69)*.

2. Containing borders are like picture frames, surrounding and holding in the quilt design *(Figure 2.29, p. 70)*.

3. Partial borders appear on some, not all, edges of the design *(Figure 2.30, p. 70)*.

Choose border measurements which are compatible with block or split-out sizes. The quilt containing 15″, 12″, 9″, and 6″ blocks could have a border based on any of those measurements, as well as the split-out sizes of 5″, 4″, 3″, and 2″. Try drawing your borders in several different ways, and then decide which of these is most visually pleasing. You can incorporate split-out units into borders, or leave uneven outside shapes created by the edges of blocks and split-outs *(Figure 2.31, p. 71)*.

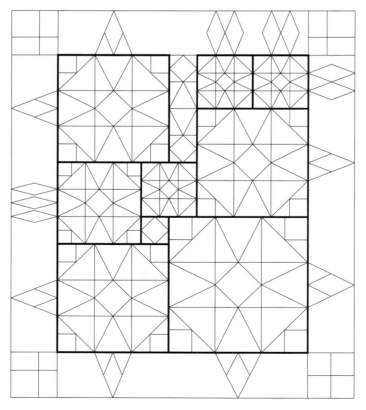

Figure 2.28: *Melded border design by Beatrice F. Johnson*

When You Wish Upon A Star by Beatrice F. Johnson, Manalapan, New Jersey. 37" x 43".

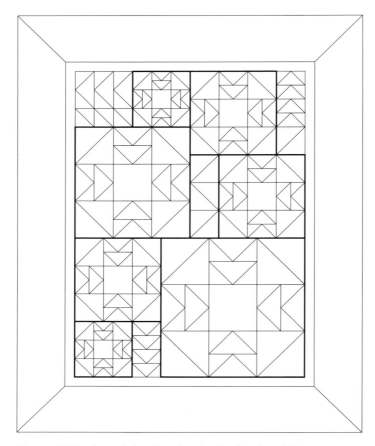

Figure 2.29: *Containing border design by Carol Boyer*

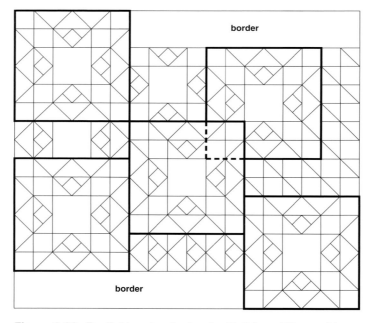

Figure 2.30: *Partial border design by Kathleen Fitzgerald*

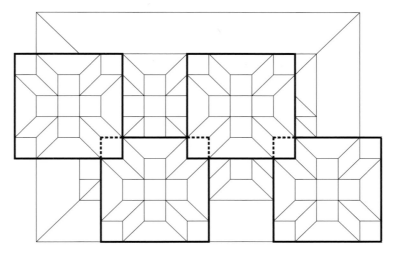

Figure 2.31: *Uneven edges*

CHANGING THE LAYOUT

Creating these designs is fun! Be willing to try more than one layout of your chosen block. Your first or second attempt will no doubt yield fine results, but you never know what else is possible until you experiment.

Change the "rules".

1. Try more than one large block.
2. Work from smallest to largest.
3. Cluster small blocks together.
4. Make the design heavier at the top.
5. Splice around the outside edge.
6. Create two distinct halves or make a triptych.
7. Feature specialty fabric in large spaces between the blocks, as in Lois Griffin's **Coney Island**. Her hand-painted fabrics wonderfully portray the smoky night sky during a fireworks display *(p. 72)*.

What if?...

If you can pull yourself away from all of these fascinating possibilities and settle on one design (for now), it's time to move on to the next milestone — an exploration of the world of color.

Coney Island by Lois Griffin, Woodbridge, New Jersey. 44" x 31".

II The Journey

COLOR

I love studying and learning about color. I hope you have discovered or are discovering the joy of color. It is not a subject which should send quilt-makers into a frenzy or make them rush from the quilt shop moaning in dismay. Instead it is like a good novel or a delicious dinner where you can progress with enjoyment from beginning to end. The best part of color study, however, is that it seems to have no end. Each new quilt offers the opportunity to refine an idea or try something totally new (and there are no dirty dishes as a result!).

SUPPORTING THE THEME

Consider again your initial motivation for this quilt. Are you portraying something or someplace specific? Have you selected a theme or mood? Whatever your plan, there are colors which are evocative to *you* of place or event or time. If you are working with a focus fabric, there are colors which will support and enhance it. Maybe you simply enjoy using certain colors and are eager to put them into a new quilt.

Most importantly, choose colors which please you and convey the message of your quilt. If there is one universal truth in quiltmaking, it is that every-one sees color differently, and that color affects everyone in different ways. Therefore, select what works for *you!*

DETERMINING COLOR PLACEMENT AND VALUE

There are many possibilities for the placement of colors in your design. The major decision you must make is whether to maintain the look of separate blocks as in Pege Fischman's **Nantucket Sunrise**, seen here, or to let the colors run over the surface of the quilt, blurring design lines, as in **Morning in an English Garden** by Bev Hertler *(p. 76)*. Both quilts achieve the desired effect.

Nantucket Sunrise by Pege Fischman, Fair Haven, New Jersey. 45" x 42".

Morning in an English Garden by Beverly Hertler, Red Bank, New Jersey. 51" x 40".

Even more important than the colors themselves are the values of those colors. Value, the relative lightness or darkness of a color, will ultimately create the motion, emphasis, or specific design which is seen in your quilt, as **Sally's Gems** by Bea Johnson beautifully illustrates below. Her use of the dark jewel tones against the pastel background results in striking visual impact. It is the contrast of lighter colors with darker colors, and not the design lines, that determines which patterns or shapes are visible.

Sally's Gems by Beatrice F. Johnson, Manalapan, New Jersey. 30" x 33".

• The higher the contrast, the more visible the shape *(Figure 3.1)*.

Figure 3.1: *Value - high contrast*

• Blending the values gives a softer edge to the progression of color or pattern *(Figure 3.2)*.

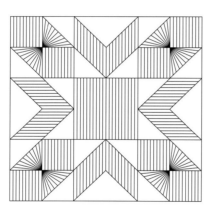
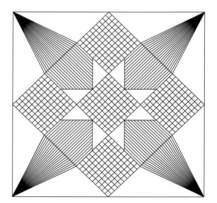

Figure 3.2: *Value - blending*

• Internal shapes in the blocks can appear or disappear simply by manipulating value *(Figure 3.3)*.

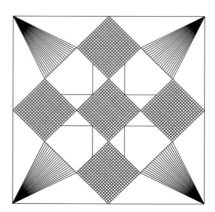

Figure 3.3: *Value - manipulating internal shapes*

DISCOVERING EMPHASIS AREAS

Let's look at one quilt design and consider the many possibilities for emphasis and color within that design. First examine the basic layout. It contains one 15″ block, three 12″ blocks, one 9″ block, and one 6″ block. The design is filled out with five 3″ square and two 6″ square split-outs *(Figure 3.4)*.

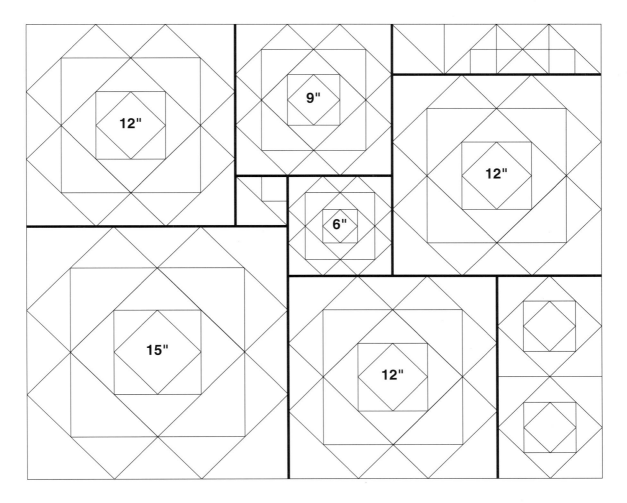

Figure 3.4: *Basic layout*

Consider some colorations of this design in its most basic form — a grouping of blocks. Here are a number of workable schemes:

- achromatic — only white, black, and gray
- monochromatic — many values of one color arranged by block or from top to bottom of the entire design
- analogous — three to five colors which touch each other in one area of the color wheel
- pure color centers surrounded by pastels
- six colors, one color per block, arranged in ascending or descending values from center to edge within each block

How many other possibilities can you think of for these blocks?

The quiltmaker's coloration of the quilt has nothing to do with the selected block design *(Figure 3.5)*. Instead Alison Curran has created an explosion of hot colors (red, orange, and yellow) in the center, surrounded by cool colors (blue, green, and violet) contained by numerous shades of black around the edges. Appropriately, she has called her quilt **Big Bang** *(p. 81)*.

Figure 3.5: *Quiltmaker's color placement.*

– – – – – – – *outside edge of hot colors*

———————— *outside edge of cool colors*

Big Bang by Alison L. Curran, Tinton Falls, New Jersey. 33" x 27".

Analyze this design further and look for different areas to emphasize. A minimum of five more possibilities can be discovered.

Let's look at variation A *(Figure 3.6A)*. The design appears to be a star on a field which rests on a background. Note that the star is not exactly dead center on the quilt and that the field has a corner missing. Design devices such as these keep your eye moving around.

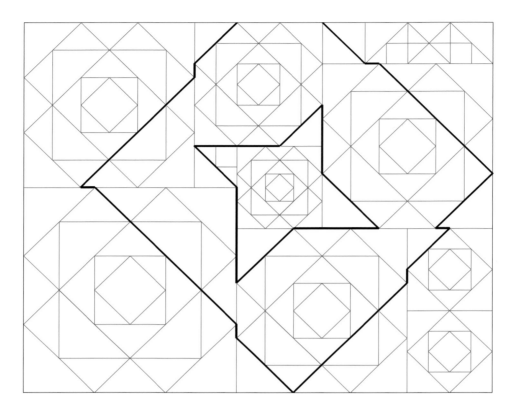

Figure 3.6A

Several color schemes are readily apparent:
• silver star, white "textured" field, shaded blue background
• gold star, red field, black background
• yellow star, shaded pink and orange field, blue background
This is just a beginning. Perhaps that star is really a black hole...

Variation B follows strong diagonals *(Figure 3.6B, p. 83)*. These diagonals could be treated in a number of ways.

 1. Make each diagonal a different color.
 2. Place a strong color in the middle, making it gradually lighter as it progresses to opposite corners.

3. Select a color on the wheel, assign it to a central diagonal, and make each successive diagonal correspond with the next color on the wheel.
4. Approach it like a colorwash. Arrange the lights and darks on each diagonal opposite to the one which touches it.

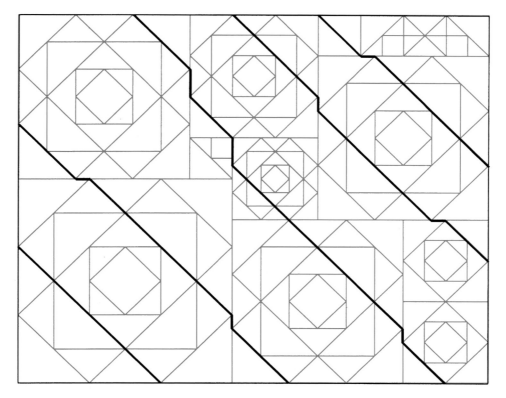

Figure 3.6B

Variation C has one focal area and two supporting areas *(Figure 3.6C, p. 84)*. Choose your colors appropriately for the "pictures" you wish to create.

1. Does it suggest a river rushing through a gorge?
2. Is the river drifting along flower-strewn mossy banks?
3. Is it a comet streaking across the night sky?
4. Do you see flaming lava coursing down a mountain?

Here are even more exciting ideas.

1. Place the lines from variation C over variation B and have a great time playing with transparency!
2. Weave the lines of C over and under the lines of B. This would be a wonderful exercise for using values...

At this rate, variations D and E may begin to seem less interesting. Not at all!

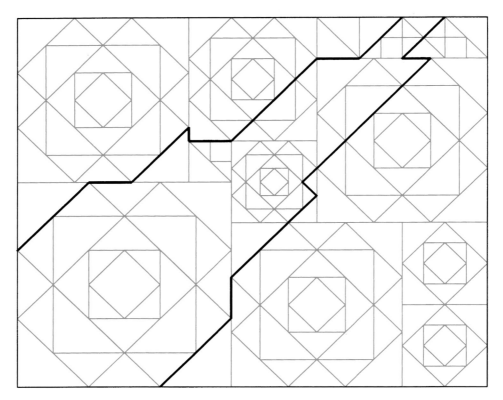

Figure 3.6C

1. Choose a focus fabric for all of the centers in D *(Figure 3.6D, p. 85)*. Support this with strong color surrounding it. Create an interesting "moving" background underneath it all. It's quite possible that the background will become the best part of the quilt.

2. Try placing rich, jewel-tone colors in the crystal-like diagonals of variation E *(Figure 3.6E, p. 85)*. Surround these with forest-green, deep-wine red, and black.

There are still more emphasis areas that you can no doubt find in this block lay-out. After all, we didn't even turn it on the side or upside down!

These variations with each of their possibilities should encourage you to look beyond your basic design.

1. Find diagonals to follow, or isolate different areas of the individual blocks. This will lead you to see your design in new ways.

2. Place tracing paper over your graph paper block layout.

3. Draw emphasis area lines based on what you are seeing.

In some ways it's like following the maze on the cereal box when you were young... or just yesterday!

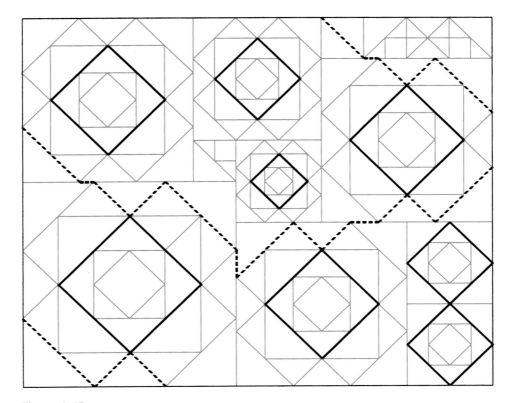

Figure 3.6D

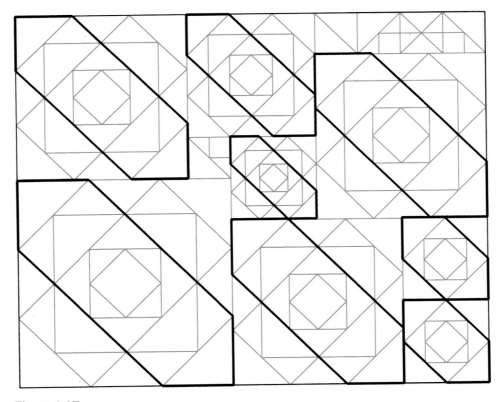

Figure 3.6E

Use **Work Station VI** to practice finding *emphasis areas.*

WORK STATION VI - EMPHASIS AREAS

Place tracing paper over the quilt design. Following lines in the design, outline different emphasis areas for each quilt. Look for:

A. centers of individual blocks

B. strong diagonals in one direction over the quilt surface

C. illusions of curves

D. strong diagonals in a V-shape over the quilt surface

E. stars, diamonds, squares

F. a central area of the whole design

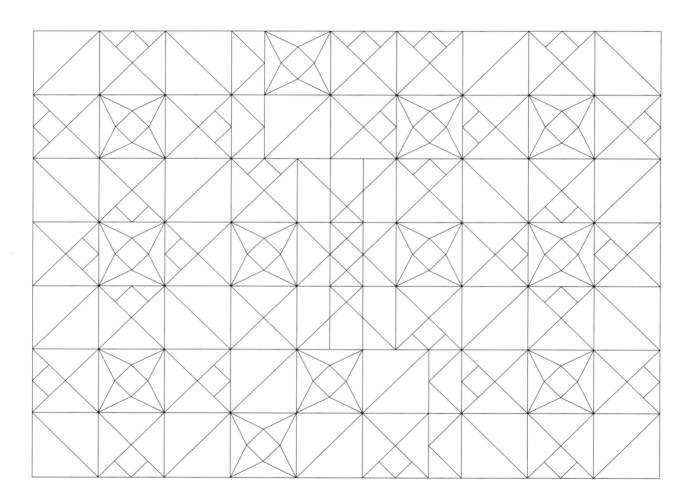

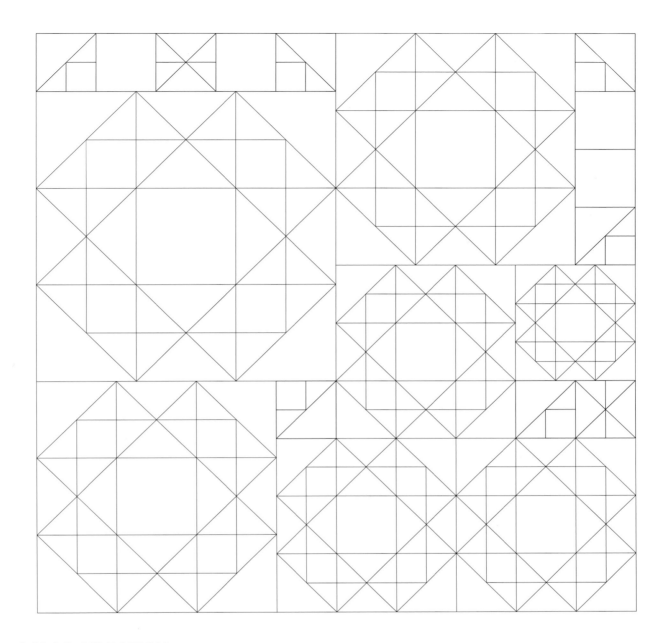

COLOR SELECTION

Remember that you had an initial motivation for your quilt. What colors do you associate with that time or place? You can begin selecting colors based on that premise. Or has the design evolved into a new life of its own and you're being taken along for the ride? Pam Buckalew began with some interesting, but not necessarily related fabrics. As she worked, with lots of input and encouragement from her friend, Betty Jane O'Donnell, the colors began to organize themselves into a suggestion of moving light. From there it was a fairly logical progression until they arrived at **Shoemaker-Levy 9** *(p. 88)*.

Shoemaker-Levy 9 by Pamela G. Buckalew, South River, New Jersey. 42" x 33".

Do you seek new color inspiration? The simplest answer is an easy one —
open your eyes and look around you.

Color is everywhere! Color, both natural and man-made, surrounds us.
Begin to collect a library of color sources: *National Geographic* magazines,
flower company catalogs, the Crate and Barrel catalog (the photography in
color groupings is wonderful), museum catalogs, travel brochures, fine art
books (look for them on remainder tables at the bookstore), postcards,
note cards, and museum posters. You'll soon have a terrific place to find
color ideas. My favorites are postcards, notecards, and catalogs because
they don't require much storage space and are easy on the budget (leaving
more funds for the fabric!).

And speaking of fabric, don't forget to look at color combinations which
you find in all kinds of fabrics, not just cottons or calicos. Fabric designers
have studied color and know how to use it. Look also at tapestries and
embroidered and knitted clothing. Look at colors used in other cultures in
their decorative arts as well as fabrics.

ANXIETY-FREE COLOR THEORY

Choosing the group of colors with which you will work is great fun.
Sometimes the selection process is purely instinctive. At other times a
basic understanding of the color wheel and both natural and art harmonies
(effective combinations of colors) can be most helpful. As with most everything in life, color is not just black or white (pun intended...). There are various color theorists and differing methods of organizing color wheels or
circles. Thankfully, however, a basic glossary of terms exists on which
most everyone can agree. According to Faber Birren, a noted color expert,
all the colors seen by the eye fall into one of these seven categories and
are represented on a triangle in the following manner *(Figure 3.7)*:

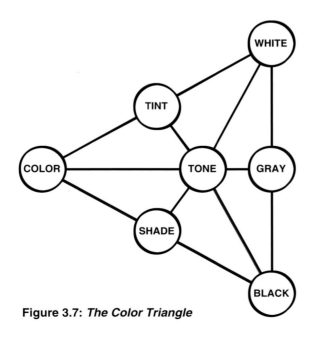

Figure 3.7: *The Color Triangle*

- color —pure colors (red, yellow, blue, green, purple... containing no white, black or gray)
- white
- black
- gray — combination of white and black
- tint — pure color mixed with white (pink, lavender, peach...)
- shade — pure color mixed with black (eggplant, navy...)
- tone — pure color mixed with white and black or gray

The remaining terms are:
- hue — the name of a color (red, orange, rose, peach...)
- value — the relative lightness or darkness of a color
- chroma — the relative purity or grayness of a color
strong chroma = pure color
weak chroma = grayed color
intensity and saturation are often synonyms for chroma

Given all of this, you need not know any of these terms to be a successful quiltmaker. However, chances are that you will be a more interesting quilt-maker with some basic color knowledge at your command.

Let's look at several different color wheels. We should remember that these were devised to organize colors in a circular sequence compatible with varying points of view. Both scientists and artists have created them based on the physics of light, pigment and dyes, and human vision. I find it useful to know about these color wheels because it gives me more options when choosing groups of colors with which I want to work. For example, you will quickly see in the Ives color wheel that what we have assumed was always the complementary color of red may not be green!

On the following pages are four wheels. You may be familiar with the arrangement of Johannes Itten, but Herbert E. Ives, Wilhelm Ostwald, and Albert Munsell offer useful color harmonies as well *(Figures 3.8 through 3.11)*.

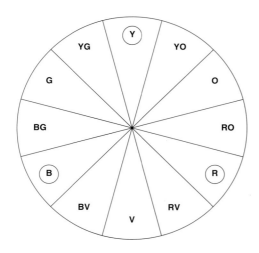

Figure 3.8: The Itten Color Circle

Yellow	**Red**	**Blue**
Yellow Orange	**Red Violet**	**Blue Green**
Orange	**Violet**	**Green**
Red Orange	**Blue Violet**	**Yellow Green**

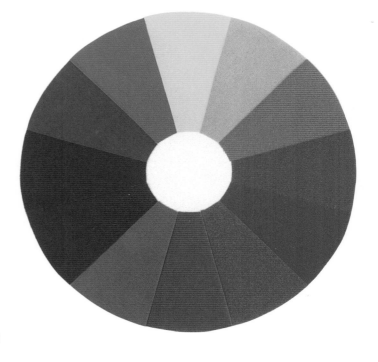

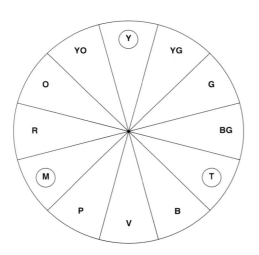

Figure 3.9: The Ives Color Circle

Yellow	**Turquoise**	**Magenta**
Yellow Green	**Blue**	**Red**
Green	**Violet**	**Orange**
Blue Green	**Purple**	**Yellow Orange**

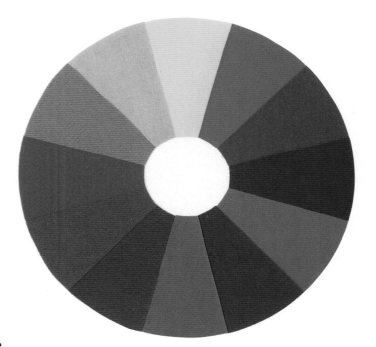

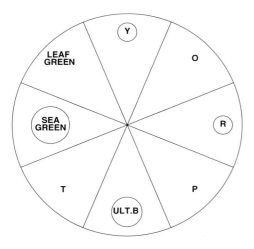

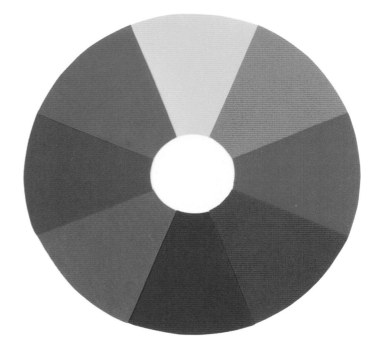

Figure 3.10: The Ostwald Color Circle

Yellow	Ultramarine Blue
Orange	Turquoise
Red	Sea Green
Purple	Leaf Green

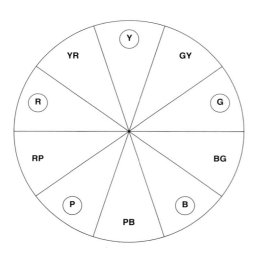

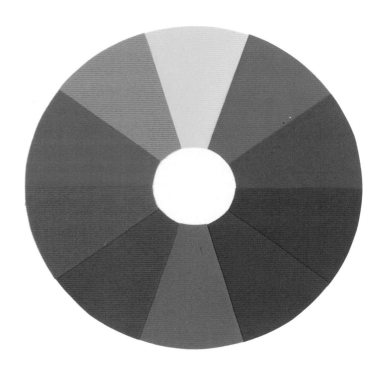

Figure 3.11: The Munsell Color Circle

Yellow	Purple Blue
Green Yellow	Purple
Green	Red Purple
Blue Green	Red
Blue	Yellow Red

PRIMARY COLORS	
Itten	red, yellow, blue
Ives	magenta, yellow, turquoise
Ostwald	red, ultramarine blue, seagreen, yellow
Munsell	red, yellow, green, blue, purple

Now we need to know briefly how we can use the color wheel to help us select color combinations, called harmonies. A short list of useful terms:
- *Analogous harmony* — those colors which touch each other in one part of the wheel and occupy less than half of the circle; using a minimum of three colors, a maximum of five.
- *Complementary harmony* — those colors located directly across the circle from each other.
- *Split Complementary harmony* — using a color and the two colors on either side of its complement; the complement is not used.
- *Double Complementary harmony* — using two colors which touch each other on the circle, plus both of their complements.
- *Triadic harmony* — using three colors spaced at equal intervals around the wheel (you can adapt this idea to work with the Ostwald and Munsell circles).
- *Tetradic harmony* — using four colors spaced at equal intervals around the wheel.

Harmonies based on color itself are given these names:
- achromatic — black, white and gray
- monochromatic — one color
- polychromatic — many colors

A fine example of analogous harmony is the color selection in Jean Markowitz's **Two Shapes, Two Colors** *(p. 94)*. She has used the colors from red violet through blue.

You have begun to explore the wonders of color. I hope it will always be fascinating. For more in-depth discussion on color related to quilt-making, I highly recommend to you my first and second favorite books on this very subject: (1) *Color and Cloth* by Mary Coyne Penders and (2) *The Magical Effects of Color* by Joen Wolfrom. There are also wonderful color/design books containing page after page of inspiring combinations. Please refer to the bibliography for additional books.

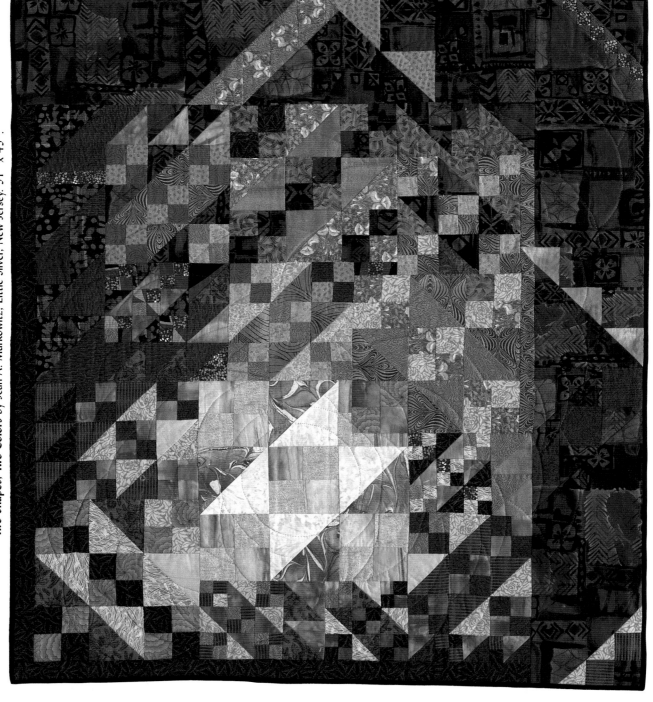

Two Shapes, Two Colors by Jean A. Markowitz, Little Silver, New Jersey. 51" x 45".

COLOR AUDITIONS

Select several groups of colors for your design and enjoy experimenting with these combinations. Try this method of using tracing paper and colored pencils to help you make choices about color groupings and placement.

Step 1: Trace over your pencil design lines on the graph paper with your fine-point black marker. This will enable you to see the design through the tracing paper which you place over it.

Step 2: With the tracing paper on top, draw in your emphasis areas (as in *Figures 3.6A-E, pp. 82-85)*. Try this step in several different ways.

Step 3: Now use the colored pencils on the tracing paper to rough out areas of color placement throughout your design. This step is not intended to be a piece-by-piece accurate representation of where each color will be placed; rather, you can quickly evaluate each trial combination and choose to set it aside or explore it further.

Note: Another method for testing emphasis areas and color would be to photocopy your design and mark the copies.

Step 4: Once you have selected a color scheme, try different shadings or value placement. Rearranging the lights, mediums, and darks can result in wonderful surprises and new ways of looking at your design.

Use **Work Station VII** on pages 96-98 to experiment with various *color harmonies.*

When you've arrived at your color selection and placement, we're ready to move on to one of the best spots on any journey — the fabric collection.

Assemble color harmonies using various fabrics. Working with the four color circles (pp. 91-92), try as many combinations as you can with as many different fabrics as you have available. You may choose to place tracing paper over the book pages and glue fabric samples to the paper for future reference.

Analogous Harmonies

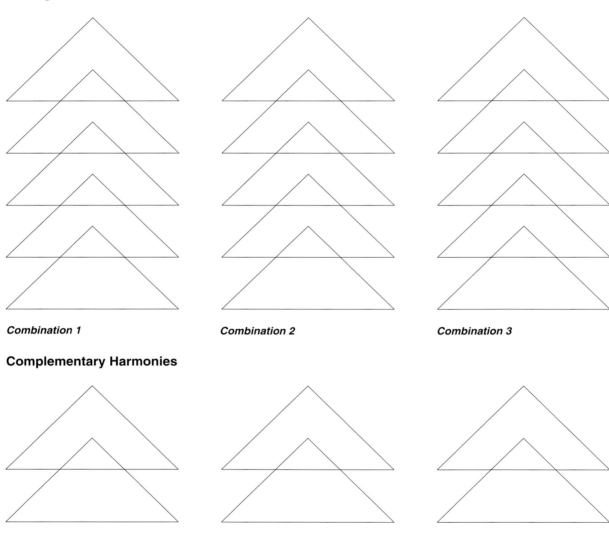

Combination 1   Combination 2   Combination 3

Complementary Harmonies

Combination 1   Combination 2   Combination 3

Split Complementary Harmonies

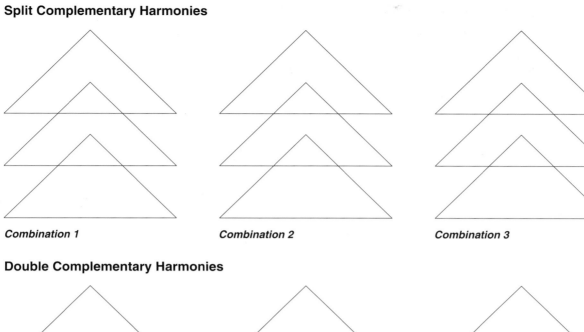

Combination 1 *Combination 2* *Combination 3*

Double Complementary Harmonies

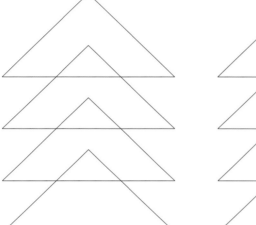
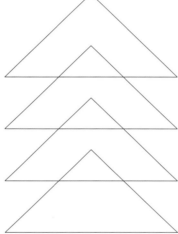
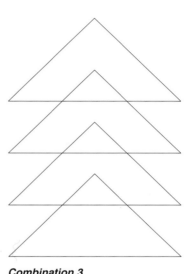

Combination 1 *Combination 2* *Combination 3*

Triadic Harmonies

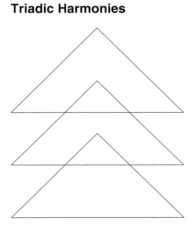
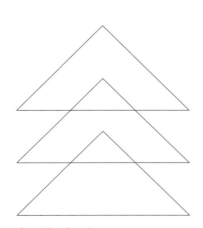
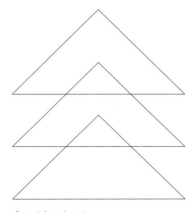

Combination 1 *Combination 2* *Combination 3*

Tetradic Harmonies

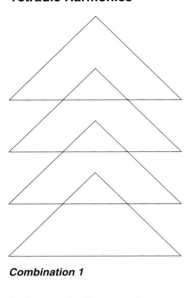

Combination 1

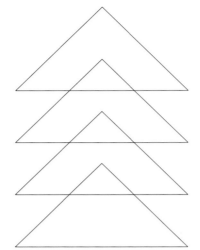

Combination 2

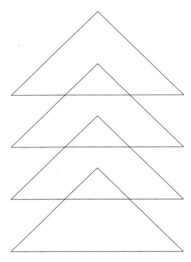

Combination 3

Achromatic Harmonies

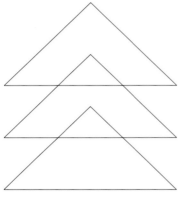

Combination 1

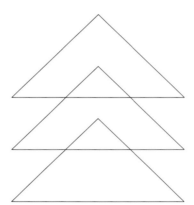

Combination 2

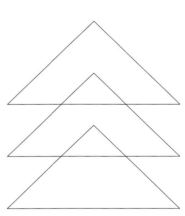

Combination 3

Monochromatic Harmonies

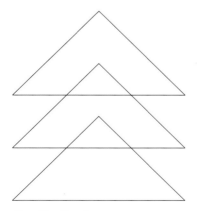

Combination 1

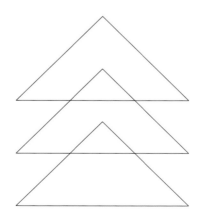

Combination 2

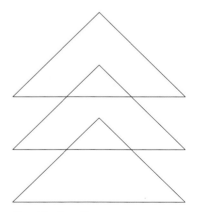

Combination 3

FABRIC

Fabric, glorious fabric! You truly can't own too much of it!! Most quilt-makers are familiar with 100% cotton fabrics and use them in their quilts. It is a sturdy, reasonable choice. For quilts which are handled frequently, it makes sense to use cloth which is washable. And today's cotton fabrics offer a wealth of color and visual texture.

CONSIDERING FABRIC TYPES

The quilts designed with this system tend to be smaller and more often displayed than handled. That allows us to consider including other types of fabrics in addition to cotton as Mary Beth Seidenfield has done in **Midnight Storm** *(p. 102)*. Drapery-weight moiré and damask as well as lamé add textural interest to her bold design. The following fabrics can be used successfully:
- drapery-weight cottons
- lamé
- silk — shantung, noil
- satin
- lightweight wool
- lightweight corduroy
- Ultrasuede®

An important consideration is to work with fabrics of similar weight. This makes the piecework much easier to handle. The use of various iron-on interfacings can help to equalize fabrics of different weights.

The advantage to including these fabrics is the amount of surface texture which they add to your design. Light is reflected differently from metallic, napped, "slick", and nubby cloth. Even though the colors in these fabrics may be similar, they will not look the same. You need not throw yourself headlong into lots of alternative fabrics at once, but be open to the opportunity of using them effectively.

GROUPING FABRICS

Once you have settled on your colors and their placement, begin to gather fabrics. You are looking for several characteristics in these fabrics:
1. colors which carry out your design
   a. art harmonies (color combinations based on use of a color wheel)
   b. natural harmonies (colors found in a particular natural setting)
   c. combinations based on emotion
   d. combinations evoking a place or time
2. variety within color groupings
   a. value — light, medium, dark
   b. pattern type
   c. pattern scale — size of design elements
   d. fabric type

Figure 4.1

Figure 4.2

Figure 4.3

Figure 4.4

Figure 4.5

Figure 4.6

Figure 4.7

Figure 4.8

Figure 4.9

Figure 4.10

Variety is a crucial consideration in your fabric selection. If you want color areas to blend across the quilt, then select similar colors as well as pattern type and scale, keeping value within a small range. For more contrast, choose fabrics with a wider span of color, pattern, and value. Either type of approach may benefit from the inclusion of "unusual" fabrics for added texture.

Following are a number of representative fabric groupings, including one of alternative types.

1. soft blues, greens; medium, medium-light value *(Figure 4.1)*
2. blues; mixed patterns; light to dark values *(Figure 4.2)*
3. gold, brown, red; interesting patterns, similar scale; medium, medium dark values *(Figure 4.3)*
4. pinks, greens; variety of scale, pattern; medium-light to medium-dark values *(Figure 4.4)*
5. monochromatic; small range of pattern scale, possible focus fabric; light to dark values *(Figure 4.5)*
6. multi-color; focus fabric, support fabric color and pattern diversity; light to dark values *(Figure 4.6)*
7. achromatic; focus fabric; pattern diversity; light to dark values *(Figure 4.7)*
8. monochromatic; natural harmony; pattern diversity; light to dark values *(Figure 4.8)*
9. polychromatic; focus fabric; pattern diversity, intense color; medium to dark values *(Figure 4.9)*
10. alternative fabrics — decorator prints, lamés, Ultrasuede®, silk, moiré, brocade, corduroy *(Figure 4.10)*

Collect a total number of fabrics between seven and twenty-five.

A word here, again, about limitations. There are those among us who can't seem to approach a project with anything less than fifty or sixty fabrics and, conversely, others who reach for five or six that are handy but totally unrelated. Let's try to find a balance between these two methods: too many fabrics only serve to confuse the issue, and too few make it difficult to carry out the design idea. Utilizing the seven to twenty-five guideline can be helpful. As you work, of course, you may add to or subtract from your original selections.

TESTING FABRIC CHOICES

A design technique which many quiltmakers find useful is to make a fabric mock-up. This enables you to see the design interpreted in fabric on a smaller scale. It will give you a sense of actual color placement and the proportion of the fabrics working together. This is a good way to see if a fabric actually will "read" in context the way that you envision it. In the case of large prints, remember that this method will only give you a hint of how the full size piece will appear.

Midnight Storm by Mary Beth Seidenfield, Short Hillsr, New Jersey. 49" x 40".

Step 1: To make a mock-up, enlarge your design.

    A. Use a copy machine

      or

    B. Re-draw it on 4 to-the-inch graph paper.

Step 2: Proceed using one of these methods.

    A. Free cut small pieces of fabric which approximate the shapes of your design.

      1. Apply glue stick to the paper design copy.

      2. Place the fabrics onto the paper.

    B. Cut 2″ square swatches of your fabrics.

      1. Apply glue stick or rubber cement to the *back* side of 4 to-the-inch graph paper.

      2. Glue the 2″ swatches of fabric *wrong* side down to the paper.

      3. Use the graph paper lines to cut accurately-sized fabric pieces.

      4. Glue these pieces to the appropriate place on your enlarged design copy.

CUTTING THE FABRICS

When you are reasonably certain of your fabric choices and their placement, you are ready to cut (gasp!) the cloth to actual size. You may go about this by using templates, quick-cutting techniques, or a combination of these methods.

Step 1: Analyze your block design and isolate the basic shapes which you will need *(Figure 4.11)*.

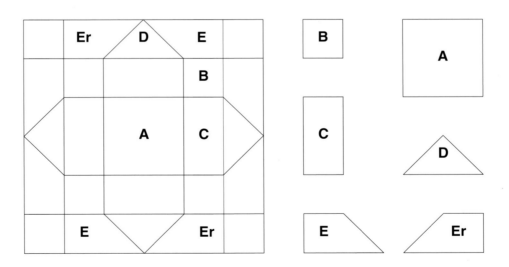

Figure 4.11: *Block shapes for templates or quick-cutting*

Step 2: Figure the sizes of each shape *(Figure 4.12)*. When in doubt, count the blocks on the graph paper. The example shows figuring shape measurements for one block in three sizes.

Figure 4.12

This chart shows finished measurements of block shapes for one block pattern in three sizes.

Add 1/4" seam allowances.

Block Sizes	12"	9"	6"
A	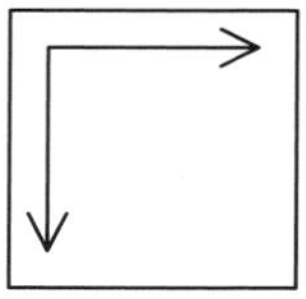 4" square	3" square	2" square
B	 2" square	$1\frac{1}{2}$" square	1" square
C	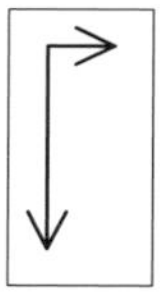 2" x 4" rectangle	$1\frac{1}{2}$" x 3" rectangle	1" x 2" rectangle
D	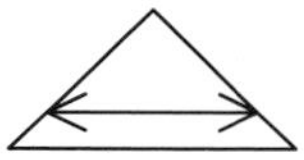 4" hypotenuse	3" hypotenuse	2" hypotenuse
E 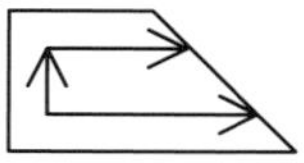 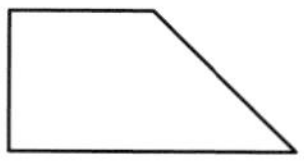 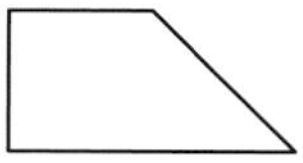 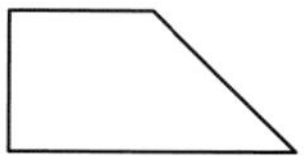	2" / 2" / 4"	$1\frac{1}{2}$" / $1\frac{1}{2}$" / 3"	1" / 1" / 2"

Shapes A through D can be quick-cut. Shape E requires a template.

Step 3: Determine which *quick-cutting* methods you can use. Squares and rectangles are easy. ***Remember to include seam allowance.*** Right or 90° triangles can be cut in one of two ways — based on the leg or side of the triangle, or based on the hypotenuse or "long" side. The leg forms one half of the square corner (90°), and the hypotenuse is the side opposite from the square corner *(Figure 4.13)*.

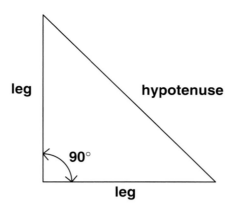

Figure 4.13: *Right triangle (90°)*

If you know the *finished* length of the leg, add 7/8″ to this measurement, cut a square of that size, and then re-cut the square once on the diagonal *(Figure 4.14, p. 106)*. This includes seam allowance.

If you know the *finished* length of the hypotenuse, add 1-1/4″ to this measurement, cut a square of that size, and then re-cut the square twice on the diagonals *(Figure 4.15, p.106)*. This includes seam allowance.

Step 4: You can make templates for all of your pieces if you wish. You will probably want templates for parallelograms or trapezoids *(Figure 4.16, p. 106)*, or other different shapes. Transparent templates of any shape are useful for isolating particular areas in your fabric which you wish to feature.

I make my templates from *accurate* 4 to-the-inch graph paper.

1. First I draw the shape I need.
2. Then, using a C-THRU® ruler with an accurate 1/4″ grid, I add the 1/4″ seam allowance all around.
   If you are hand piecing, do not add the 1/4″ to your templates.
3. To cut out these templates, I use a method which I learned from Patricia Morris, well-known quilting teacher, judge, and lecturer. You have probably always cut around a shape, holding that shape as you cut. With Pat's method you do the reverse. This moves the line to be cut *between* your eyes and the scissor blade, instead of keeping the line *behind* the blade.
   A. Hold *the area to be cut away* from the template, *instead* of the template itself.
   B. Watch the scissor blades just shave away the outside line of the seam allowance.

Therefore when you draw or cut around this template, the pencil or rotary blade is recreating the placement of that line, not adding more to the size. Try it!

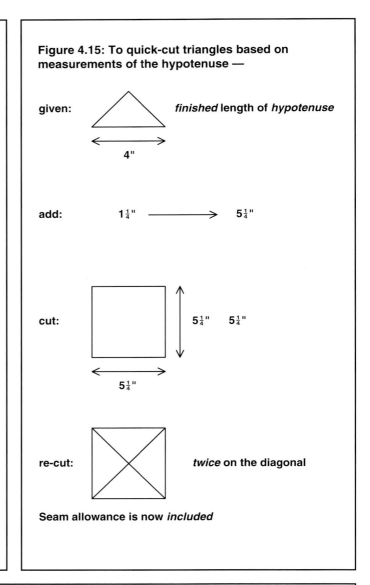

Figure 4.14: To quick-cut triangles based on measurements of the leg —

given: *finished* length of *leg*

3"

add: $\frac{7}{8}$" ⟶ $3\frac{7}{8}$"

cut: $3\frac{7}{8}$" square

$3\frac{7}{8}$"

re-cut: *once* on the diagonal

Seam allowance is now *included*

Figure 4.15: To quick-cut triangles based on measurements of the hypotenuse —

given: *finished* length of *hypotenuse*

4"

add: $1\frac{1}{4}$" ⟶ $5\frac{1}{4}$"

cut: $5\frac{1}{4}$" $5\frac{1}{4}$"

$5\frac{1}{4}$"

re-cut: *twice* on the diagonal

Seam allowance is now *included*

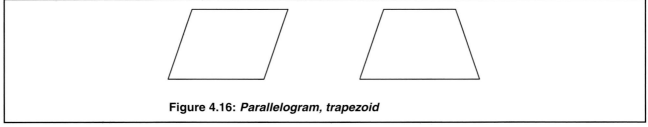

Figure 4.16: *Parallelogram, trapezoid*

4. If I need a plastic template, I still draw the shape on graph paper first. Then I transfer it to the plastic and cut, using Pat's method.

To hold the templates in place on my fabrics, I make small circles of 1/4″ masking tape and place them strategically on the back of the template. Small, self-adhesive sandpaper dots or strips also work well. Then I can line up the edge of a small rotary ruler placed on top of the template and cut each side. When I feel like living dangerously, I simply cut around the paper template — *very* carefully!

MAKING AND USING A DESIGN WALL

Because most of these quilts will live on a wall, it is of utmost importance to work with a design wall. You can make this vital aid for visualizing your quilt in one of the following ways.

1. Tape a piece of *white* felt, flannel, or fleece to a door or wall. 1-1/4 yards of material will give you at least a 45″ square work area.
2. Cover a large piece of foam core board or a panel of styrofoam insulation with *white* felt.
3. For a permanent wall space, 4 ft. x 7 ft. sheets of wallboard, covered with *white* felt or flannel, make a wonderful design wall onto which you may pin fabric pieces.

You need the perspective of seeing these fabrics work together in an upright position. You can work on a floor or table, but then you must stand on a chair or ladder as you go along. A reducing glass (makes things smaller rather than magnifying), a peep-hole mechanism for a door (available at your builder's supply — thank you, Natasha!), or looking through your camera viewfinder or the wrong end of your binoculars will help you get a long-distance view in a small space.

As you cut your pieces, put them in place on the design wall.

1. Watch how the fabrics interact.
2. Are the fabrics working to bring your design to life?
3. Are they blending or colliding?
4. What is the effect that you want these pieces of cloth to create?

In the best of all possible worlds, your selected fabrics will be perfect — and sometimes that "magic" happens!

In the real world, however, there may be one or two (or even most of them) that just aren't working. When you set about changing these "wayward children", do so gradually.

1. Each change that you make will affect how the other fabrics look and relate to one another.
2. Audition new candidates one at a time by cutting one or several pieces and observing the interaction with the total look of the quilt.
3. Look and "listen". The quilt and your intuition will tell you when you've got it right.

Don't toss the pieces which you have removed from this quilt! Add them to the scrap bag, box, or drawer. Someday they will be just the pieces you need and you'll be glad to find them.

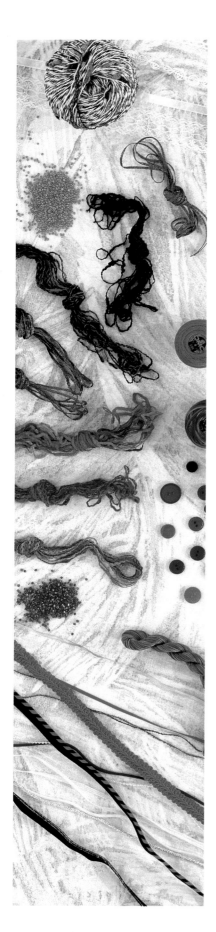

STITCHING THE TOP

When you are satisfied with all of your fabric placement, it's time to sew the pieces together. Consult your layout and review your construction plan. If you are adding borders to a central pieced area, *please* measure the piecework, along horizontal and vertical seams on the sides of the quilt, and cut the borders to fit *before* you sew. Don't just take lengths of cloth and stitch them on until you come to an end. In order to lay flat, the opposite borders must be equal in length.

Congratulations! You've reached an important juncture in your design journey. You can now choose the scenic route or the more direct route to your journey's end. The scenic route takes us through the wonderland of surface ornamentation. Those of you on the faster track may want to head for The Other Half *(p. 116)...*

SURFACE ORNAMENTATION

You may choose to enhance your piecework design in numerous ways. A cautionary note here — these options are loads of fun to consider and carry out. I recommend that you plan ahead for spending a fair amount of time in this wonderland!

The possibilities are these:
- basic appliqué
- dimensional appliqué
- dimensional piecework
- trims
- embroidery
- "stardust"

The first important decision to be made with regard to surface ornamentation is whether you quilt before or after something is applied to the quilt top. You may also quilt as you apply items. It depends on your preference and the type of quilting (hand, machine) which you select. Consider the difficulty in maneuvering around or through the ornamentation and make your decision accordingly.

Let's examine how these can be used on your one-of-a-kind design.

OVERLAYING APPLIQUÉ

The first choice is to stitch flat appliqués onto particular areas of your design.
- flowers
- vines and leaves
- houses
- animals
- hearts
- hands
- fish
- trees
- vehicles
- birds
- stars
- and...

A flower or pattern which appears in your fabrics could be interpreted on a larger scale through appliqué — either once or several times over the quilt top.

The pieced design can function as a background environment for appliqués. In **The Superstitions** *(p. 110)*, King's Crown blocks are set on point, and hand-painted as well as commercially printed fabrics are used to create the illusion of sky, mountains, and desert. This becomes a backdrop for the appliquéd animals and plants. There are natural combinations which you might try:
• salt water — fish, seaweed, coral
• icy Antarctica — penguins
• pond, lake or river — turtles, frogs
• Southwestern desert — cactus, lizards, snakes
• mountains — trees, rocks

WORKING WITH DIMENSION

Dimensional appliqué adds interest as **A Secret Garden for My Friend** *(p. 111)* illustrates. Claudia Menendez designed and stitched the "trellis" background onto which she and fellow teacher, Janet Spencer, appliquéd the vines and leaves. Design and stitch your background; then
• create stuffed flowers, fruit, leaves
• stitch gathered, ruched, or ribbon flowers
• layer fabrics to build up larger shapes
• make fabric tubes; weave them together and stitch down over the surface of the quilt
• sew faced shapes; apply to quilt surface with a tuck, twist, or turn, making both sides visible.

Dimensional piecework incorporates shapes such as prairie points or scallops:
• sewn into the seams to define an emphasis area
• sewn across the quilt surface to scatter sparkle or create subtle color change.

Use two-sided flaps which can be rearranged by turning them to one side or the other. Hold them in place with buttons, snaps, or velcro. These flaps will change color, reveal hidden treasures, or create totally new patterns. The fasteners become part of the design as well.

If you were really ambitious, you might incorporate zippered areas which open to reveal surprises, or pockets containing...

TRIMMINGS

Trimmings of all kinds, shapes, sizes, and colors present fascinating embellishment possibilities. The list includes yarns, ribbons, braids, fringe, lace, eyelet, and heavier decorative threads.

The Superstitions by Lynn G. Kough, Middletown, New Jersey. 29" x 36".

A Secret Garden for My Friend by Claudia Menendez, North Plainfield, New Jersey, 45" x 36".

Yarns, both exotic and novelty, can be used "as is" or taken apart, with selected strands stitched separately.

Ribbons (woven silk, satin, or grosgrain — not craft) offer exciting possibilities. They are:

- flexible
- crushable
- knot-able
- weave-able
- twistable
- braidable
- bunchable
- and, of course, stitchable.

Braids are available in an amazing variety: rick-rack, piping, flat, and cording.

From plain colors to multi-color to metallics, the versatility of braids is wonderful. Lynn Liebenow's **Rosie May** *(p. 113)* not only successfully blends an interesting group of fabrics, but also makes effective use of gold braid echoing the rose print featured in the quilt. Handle braids in any number of ways:

- Stitch into seams
- Couch on top
- Twist, then topstitch
- Manipulate, then hand-tack in place.

Fringe may be limited in its appeal to a quiltmaker, but you're creative — you'll think of something! It would certainly be appropriate for a Victorian or Western look.

Lace, netting or *tulle*, and *eyelet* all offer embellishment possibilities. These may be layered into or on top of the piecework. Smaller versions with finished edges can be topstitched.

Heavier threads, intended mostly for sergers, make fine couched designs. Or use them to create your own yarns by twisting or braiding several kinds together.

CONSIDERING EMBROIDERY

Next consider embroidery for embellishing your quilt. We have arrived at another of my favorite places — thread "heaven"! Threads, threads (plain and variegated), and more threads:

- cotton
- silk
- metallic
- rayon
- polyester
- blends

Both hand and machine embroidery can personalize your design, add interest, and challenge your creativity. New advances in needle construction for the sewing machine make embroidery work with special threads more satisfying. Embroidery floss, ribbon floss, and lightweight silk ribbon offer possibilities for hand stitching.

Rosie May by Mary Lynn Liebenow, Holmdel, New Jersey; 38" x 32".

ADDING STARDUST

Last, but far from least, we reach a very special place on our journey through embellishment wonderland. I call these materials "stardust". This is the home of buttons, beads, bangles, baubles, and glitz. Here reside both the sublime and the ridiculous, the fine and the funky! A veritable treasure trove of trinkets awaits you:

- beads: seed, rocaille, bugle glass, clay, wood, plastic, metal
- pearls
- buttons: plastic, mother-of-pearl, glass, clay, wood, metal, cloth covered, yarn, thread-woven, knotted
- sequins: flat, cup, shapes
- metal studs
- rhinestones
- charms

Debbie Davies uses some delightful "stardust" on her wonderful quilt, **Genesis 1:20** *(quilt on p. 115, detail below)*. These bits of whimsey are a finishing touch right in character with her fabric choices.

You can also use found objects and natural goodies, such as shells, by gluing earring posts to them. This will pierce the quilt, and then the backing piece will hold the object in place.

Truth to tell, there are many more possibilities for embellishing your quilt. A number of additional sources, both ideas and items, are listed in the appendix. Enjoy your exploration!

Genesis 1:20 by Deborah Davies, Freehold, New Jersey. 33" x 45".

 The Destination

THE OTHER HALF

Have you ever felt that great sense of accomplishment when you finished stitching together the top of your quilt, followed shortly by the realization that there remained a great deal to be done before it really was a quilt? Haven't we all! But completing the "other half" of your quilt can be a fine journey also. These are the remaining guideposts:

- Planning, cutting, and stitching the backing
- Selecting and preparing the batting
- Planning and stitching the quilting design
- Finishing the edges
- Labeling your quilt

MAKING THE BACKING

After you have put so much thought, time, and effort into the top of your quilt, don't skimp on the back. Georgette Keenan carried both design and color to the back of her quilt, **It Is Over** *(p. 117)*. Those elements plus an explanatory label truly *complete* the quilt.

Choose a fabric worthy of your design — one which harmonizes with your color selection and is consistent with your primary fabrics. Here are some possibilities:

- Repeat a fabric used in the top.
- Repeat your focus fabric.
- Use a solid color which figures prominently in your design.
- Choose a similar fabric to your focus fabric, but larger or smaller in pattern scale

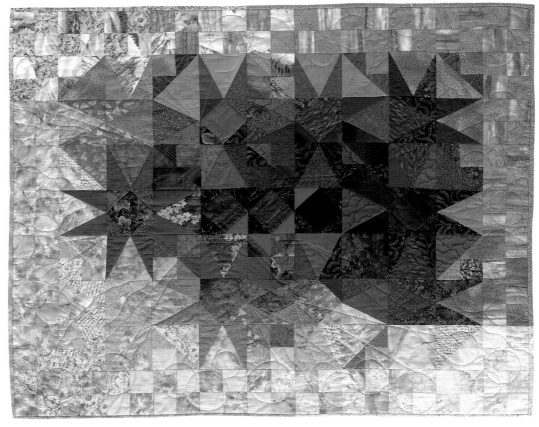

It Is Over by Georgette Keenan, Clarksburg, New Jersey. 36" x 44". Front (L) and Back (R).

- Choose a contrasting color which sets off the design colors.
- Reinforce the most important design color with the backing fabric.

You may also choose to piece several fabrics together for your backing.

1. Stitch strips, squares, or triangles representing a cross-section of the design fabrics.
2. Incorporate a block pieced exactly as it appears on the quilt top.
3. Expand the basic block until it becomes the size of the back.
4. Use two large blocks to form the back.
5. Recreate the emphasis areas in whole cloth.

Once you have decided on your backing treatment, cut and piece the fabrics. Remember to make the backing several inches larger all around than the quilt top. Press it and set it aside until you are ready to layer the quilt "sandwich".

SELECTING BATTING

Select a batting which best suits (1) the way in which this quilt will be used and (2) your method of quilting. Basically you will work with one of three fiber types:

- polyester
- cotton
- a blended batt

Wool or silk are available but less reasonable choices. For a wall quilt, choose a thin, flat batting which will hang straight. A throw or small bed quilt may require a batting with higher loft. These battings are recommended for your consideration.

- Hobbs
  — Poly-down®
  — Heirloom Cotton Batting (80% cotton, 20% polyester)
  — Thermore®

- Fairfield
  — Poly-fil® Low-Loft Batting
  — Poly-fil® Traditional Batting
  — Cotton Classic® Blend Batting (80% cotton, 20% polyester)

- Mountain Mist®
  — QUILT-LIGHT®
  — Quality Quilt Batting
  — Blue Ribbon Cotton Batting

- Warm Products, Inc.
  — Warm and Natural™ (cotton needlepunched to polyester mesh)

- Freudenberg Nonwovens
  — Pellon® Lofty Fleece

Remember to follow the manufacturer's guidelines and prepare the batting before you use it.

For hand quilting, the polyester batts and the Heirloom Cotton are probably the easiest to needle. I prefer cotton batting for machine quilting because the layers of my quilts slip and slide less as I work them through the machine. I also find that cotton batting tends to hang well.

It is a good idea to collect small amounts of many different kinds of batting and test them in various ways. This is something which can be done over a period of time. Try the batt with both hand and machine quilting.

1. Is it easy to needle?
2. Observe how it handles lots of stitching. Is it stiff or does it drape nicely?
3. Does it result in a flat edge on the quilt or does it ripple?
4. Does it hang straight and flat?

In this way you can determine which batting you want to use for a particular quilt.

PLANNING AND STITCHING THE QUILTING DESIGN

Design your quilting pattern(s) based on one of three considerations.

1. Will the quilting highlight individual elements within the overall design?
2. Will the quilting be determined by the various emphasis areas?
3. Should the quilting be an overall design which functions more to hold the quilt together than to highlight any particular area?

The quilting should become part of the whole design, either adding another element or supporting what already exists. The quilting should not appear to be an afterthought or "better than nothing"!

Do keep in mind how much of the quilting pattern will be visible after it's stitched. Consider how much time and effort you wish to expend on something which may be virtually invisible when completed.

Machine quilters should design their pattern with an eye to how many stitching lines will begin or end anywhere but at the edges of the quilt. To achieve consistency of stitch size, you will need to tie off any ends, rather than backstitching or using very small stitches. Settle on the method which best suits you.

Also remember to plan an adequate amount of quilting. A few lines here and there won't be enough. To test this, close your hand and make a fist. Then randomly place your fist all over the quilt top. Each time you set it down, you should touch at least one line of quilting stitches. If not — add more!

Quilting designs for these wall hangings fall into six general categories:

- ditch and gridwork (sounds like a heavy construction crew!)
  — stitching along seamlines
  — stitching along lines of emphasis areas
  — overlaying lines of stitching which form squares, diamonds, or triangles

- meander or stipple
  — stitching undulating lines which appear to have no beginning or end to give texture over the entire surface or in selected areas
  — repetitive fillers
  — stitching repeated shapes in particular areas (similar to meander, but the shapes are defined)
  — following a pattern printed on a fabric
  — using Sashiko designs

- 1/4″ or continuous curve
  — stitching within a pieced shape at 1/4″ from the seamlines all around the shape

- patterns
  — stitching representative shapes or geometric designs such as flowers, hearts, stars, interlocked circles, etc.
  — using decorative machine stitches

- borderwork
  — filling the frame around the quilt with linear designs such as cables, vines, zig-zags, swags, ribbons

Marking a quilting pattern on your finished top can be a tricky business. Choose your marking tool carefully. Again, there are a number of products available. I strongly recommend testing them for "removability" on the fabrics which they will mark.

My personal preference is the chalk pencil which can be sponged or soaked out of the fabric. It is available in white, red, green, and blue. The brand is marked either *Quilter's Rule Chalk Pencil* or *Dixon Washout Cloth Marker*. It requires a large hole, short barrel pencil sharpener which has a very sharp blade. You need to mark only small areas of the quilt at one time because the pattern can rub off as you handle it. I am more than willing to deal with these factors, given the knowledge that it has always come *completely* out of the fabric. To me, that quality overrides every other consideration.

Choice of thread for quilting is no longer limited to off-white or cotton. Consider what is available to you, and if possible, test types and colors against your fabrics. Each thread has a characteristic which will be useful for a particular quilt. The possibilities include:

- 100% cotton
- cotton-wrapped polyester
- rayon
- metallic
- transparent nylon, polyester

Within each variety, there are numerous brands. Again, testing these will help you to decide which one will be appropriate.

Regardless of whether you will hand or machine quilt, take the time to properly baste your quilt "sandwich". Stretching the backing taut before layering on the batting and top can make a great difference in the finished appearance of your quilt. Proper basting takes time, but the result makes it worth every minute.

FINISHING THE EDGES

The edge of your quilt should be consistent with your overall design. Consider a number of options, such as:

- binding
- facing
- prairie points, scallops
- trims — lace, ribbon, eyelet
- faced shapes
- overcast, serged
- turned in
- turned over — front to back, back to front

Whichever method you select should be in keeping with the rest of the quilt. Now is not the time for expedience!

LABELING THE QUILT

The conclusion of this design journey is at hand. It is most important that you label your work. Whether you ink or embroider your name and the date on the front, or create an elaborate one-of-a-kind tag for the back, don't neglect this important last step. If you would like some professional help for your label, there are stamps and preprinted fabrics available, as well as several good books which are listed in the bibliography.

ARRIVAL

You did it! You created an original. Congratulations! I hope you have enjoyed your journey in search of a new image for your traditional quilt, and that you will travel this road many more times. Perhaps we'll meet along the way.

Now — *What if?...*

IV | Projects and Patterns

GENERAL DIRECTIONS FOR PATTERNS

You may recreate the quilts shown in this section by using similar or different fabrics. If you wish to go off in your own direction, you might begin by looking for new emphasis areas within the design.

In the complete pattern illustration, bold lines indicate full blocks, and dashed lines indicate spliced blocks. Split-outs shown with dashed lines were formed by adding grid lines back into the block design.

First, cut your fabrics, block by block or area by area. Use either the templates printed at the end of this section *(beginning on p.149)*, or one of the quick cutting methods shown on page 148. Put the fabric pieces on your design wall as you work.

When all of the fabrics have been cut and placed, consult the quilt construction diagram and proceed in this manner:

1. Stitch the smallest units (portions of blocks, split-outs) together.

2. Stitch these units into blocks or larger areas.

3. Stitch the larger areas together until the piece is completely assembled.

4. Add borders, unless they are already incorporated into larger areas.

Stitching in numbered order means the following:

1. For units and blocks, begin with piece #1, add all #2 pieces, add all #3 pieces, and so on.

2. For construction seams, begin with seam #1, and stitch in the direction of the arrow; move to seam #2, continuing in this manner.

Border measurements are given in *finished* sizes.

Split-out measurements are given in *finished* sizes.

Since you will be using a number of fabrics, follow these general guidelines for amounts:

1. For a small quilt top (150″ circumference or smaller), 1/4 yard each of seven fabrics should suffice.

2. Using more fabrics requires smaller amounts of each, except for a focus fabric, which you will probably use in larger amounts.

3. Larger quilt tops require anywhere from 1/8 to 1/2 yard per fabric. Amounts are relative to how much of a particular fabric is used, and how many total fabrics are used.

Pattern 1: **Butterscotch** by Marjorie Johnson, Oceanport, New Jersey, 33" x 27".

Pattern 1: *Alison's design – Butterscotch (33" x 27")*

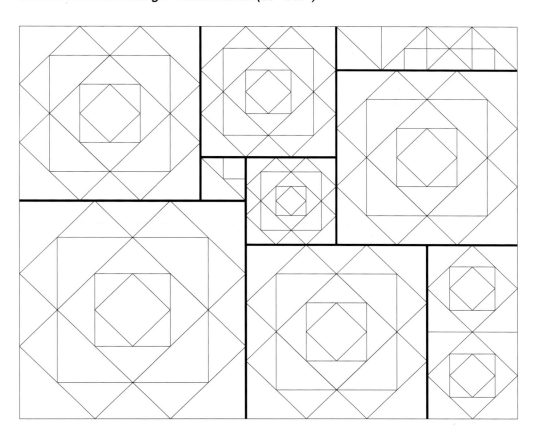

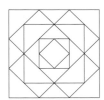

Block: Var. Gentleman's Fancy

Block sizes: 15", 12", 9", 6"

Split-outs for this design:

Pattern 1 Block

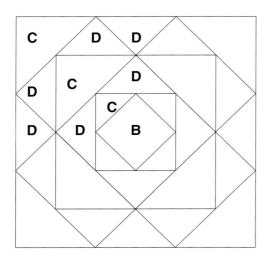

Block Size	Templates
15″	B5 C5, C2-1/2 D5
12″	B4 C4, C2 D4
9″	B3 C3, C1-1/2 D3
6″	B2 C2, C1 D2
Consult the quick-cutting chart on page 148 for C and D pieces, if desired.	

Remember:
As block sizes change, the template letter remains constant. Template numbers reflect block size changes.

Templates can be found on pages 149-151.

Pattern 1 Split-outs

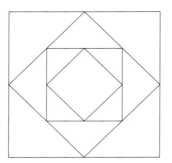

6" finished
B3, C3, C1-1/2, D3

3" finished
A1-1/2, C1-1/2, C3, D3

Pattern 1 Block Construction

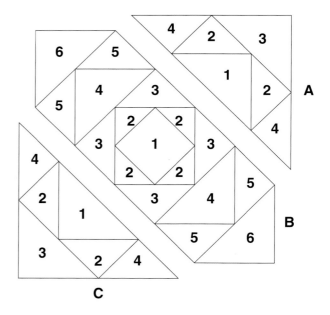

1. Sew Sections A, B, and C, adding and stitching the pieces in the numbered order.
2. Sew Sections A and C to Section B.

Pattern 1: *Butterscotch (33" x 27")*

Construction areas

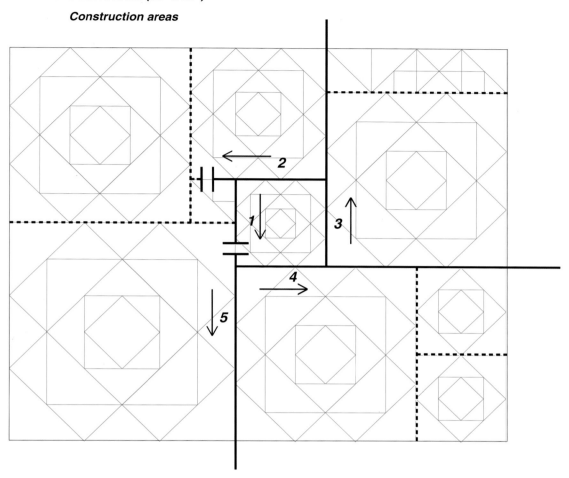

A: ------------ *stitch these units into larger units.*

B: ————————— *stitch larger areas together using partial seams around the center 6" block in numbered order.*

——|—|—— *partial seams*

Pattern 2: **A New Beginning** by Anne Marie Steeneck, Freehold, New Jersey, 28″ x 28″.

Pattern 2: *Anne Marie's design – A New Beginning (28" x 28")*

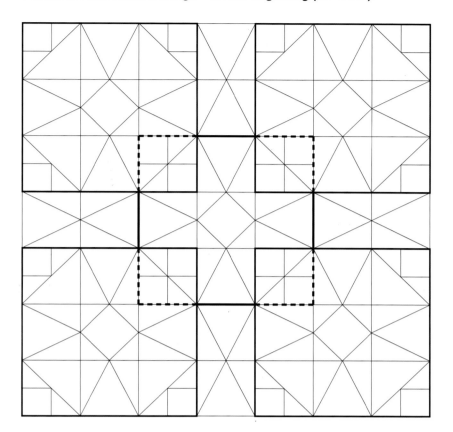

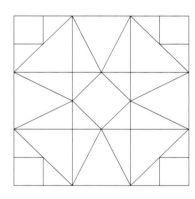

Block: Storm at Sea

Block size: 12"

Split-out for this design:

Pattern 2 Block

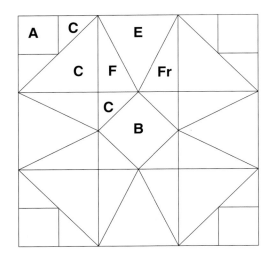
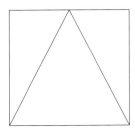

Pattern 2 Split-outs

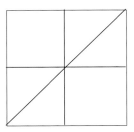

4" finished
E4, F-Fr4

4" finished
A2, C2

The "r" designation means a REVERSE template.

Block Size	Templates
12″	A2 B4 C4, C2 E4 F4
Consult the quick-cutting chart on page 148 for A and C pieces, if desired.	

Remember:
As block sizes change, the template letter remains constant. Template numbers reflect block size changes.

Templates can be found on pages 149-151.

Pattern 2 Block Construction

1. Stitch the small units together in the numbered order.

2. This quilt is constructed with long horizontal rows.
   Stitch the smaller units into rows.
   Stitch the rows together.

Pattern 2: *A New Beginning (28" x 28")*

       Construction areas

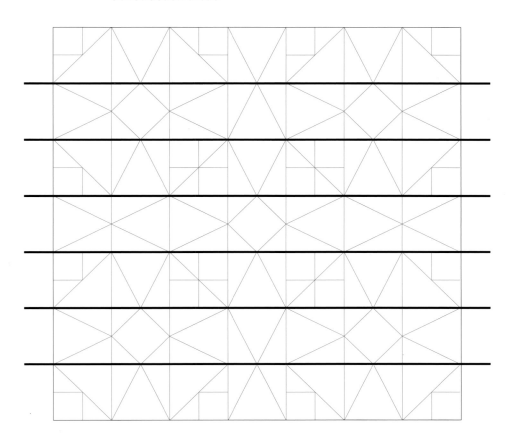

—————————— *stitch together long horizontal units.*

Pattern 3: **The Fitzies** by Kathleen Fitzgerald, Red Bank, New Jersey, 36″ x 32″.

Pattern 3: *Kate's design – The Fitzies (36" x 32")*

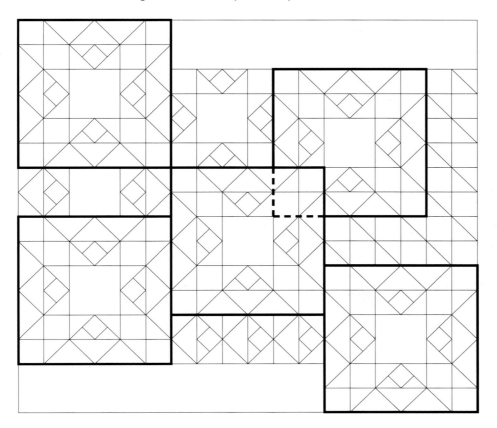

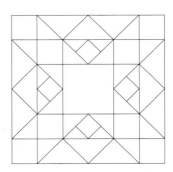

Block: Best of All

Block size: 12"

Split-outs for this design:

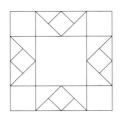

Pattern 3 Block

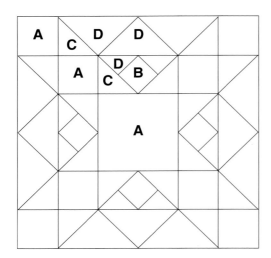

Block Size	Templates
12″	A2, A4 B2 C2 D2, D4
Consult the quick-cutting chart on page 148 for A, C, and D pieces, if desired.	

Pattern 3 Split-outs

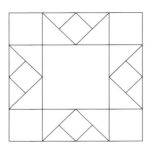

8" finished
A2, A4, B2, C2, D2

4" finished
A4, A2, B2, C2, D2, D4

Remember:
As block sizes change, the template letter remains constant. Template numbers reflect block size changes.

Templates can be found on pages 149-151.

Pattern 3 Block Construction

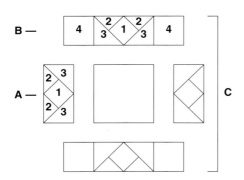

1. Stitch the center section C together, joining section A and B (x2).

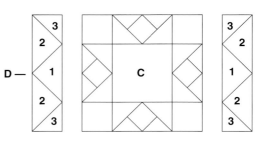

2. Add D (x2) to the completed C.

3. Add E (x2) to finish the block.

Pattern 3: *The Fitzies (36" x 32")*

      Border measurements; Construction areas

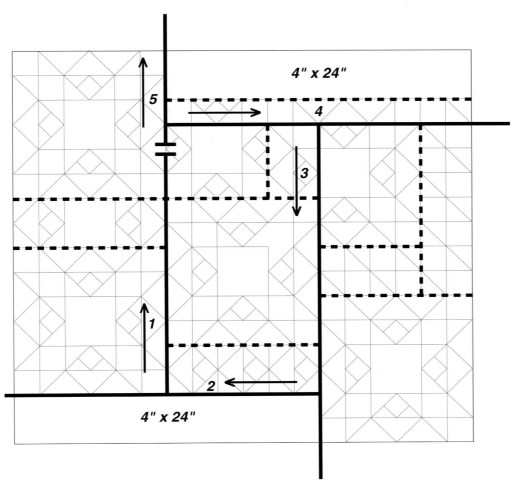

4" x 24"

4" x 24"

A: - - - - - - - -   *stitch these units into larger units.*

B: ——————   *stitch larger areas together, using a partial seam, in numbered order.*

—| |——   *partial seams*

Pattern 4: **KathAnne's Ragtime Band** by Lynn G. Kough, Middletown, New Jersey, 32″ x 28″.

Pattern 4: *Anne's design – KathAnn's Ragtime Band (32" x 28")*

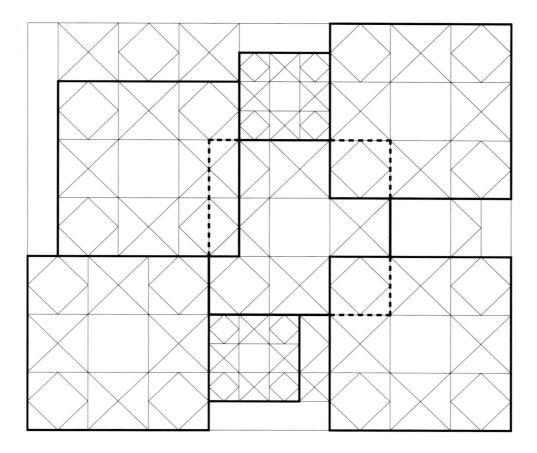

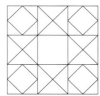

Block: Sawtooth Patchwork

Block sizes: 12", 6"

Split-outs for this design:

Pattern 4 Block

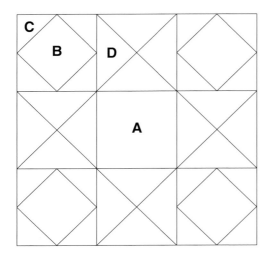

Block Size	Templates
12″	A4 B4 C2 D4
6″	A2 B2 C1 D2
Consult the quick-cutting chart on page 148 for A, C, and D, if desired.	

Remember:
As block sizes change, the template letter remains constant. Template numbers reflect block size changes.

Templates can be found on pages 149-151.

Pattern 4 Split-outs

 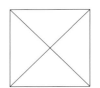

4" finished
A4, B4, C2, D4

4" x 2" finished   **2" finished**
C2, D4   **D2**

Pattern 4 Block Construction

1. This quilt is constructed by arranging smaller units into larger areas – some are complete blocks, some are not.

2. Stitch all small units first in numbered order.

3. When constructing larger areas, add in partial border units when appropriate.

Pattern 4: *KathAnn's Ragtime Band (32" x 28")*

Border measurements; construction areas

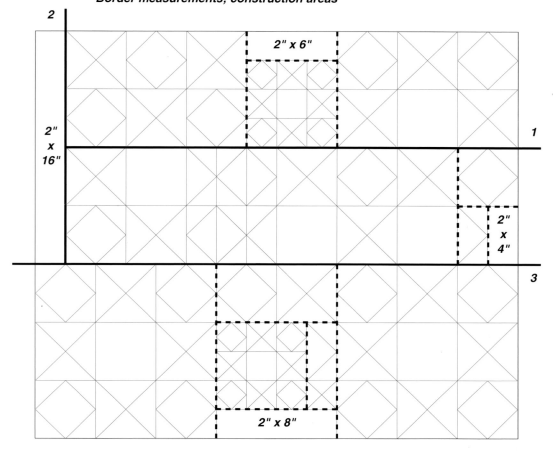

A: - - - - - - - - -   *stitch small units into larger areas.*

B: ——————————   *stitch larger areas together.*

Pattern 5: **Some Like It Hot** by Bonnie Adams, Edison, New Jersey, 36″ x 36″.

Pattern 5: *Bonnie's design – Some Like It Hot (36" x 36")*

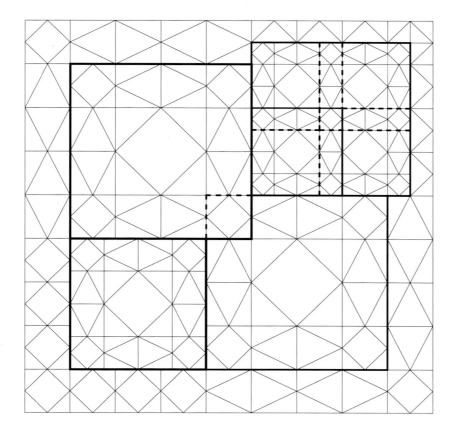

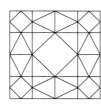

Block: Storm at Sea

Block size: 16", 12", 8"

Split-outs for this design:

Pattern 5 Block

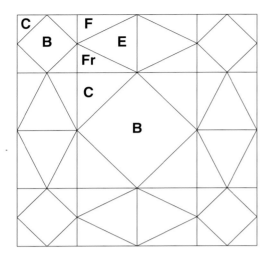

Block Size	Templates
16″	B8, B4 C4, C2 E4 F - Fr4
12″	B6, B3 C3, C1-1/2 E3 F - Fr3
8″	B4, B2 C2, C1 E2 F - Fr2
Consult the quick-cutting chart on page 148 for C if desired.	

Remember:
As block sizes change, the template letter remains constant. Template numbers reflect block size changes.

Templates can be found on pages 149-151.

Pattern 5 Split-outs

4" finished
B4, C2, E4, F-Fr4

The "r" designation means a REVERSE template.

2" x 4" finished
D4, C2

2" finished
C2

Pattern 5 Block Construction

1. The blocks and borders for this quilt are constructed (with the exception of 9 border units) from these two units.

2. Stitch them together in numbered order.

3. Assemble larger areas.

6 border units   **3 border units**

Pattern 5: *Some Like It Hot (36" x 36")*

         Construction areas

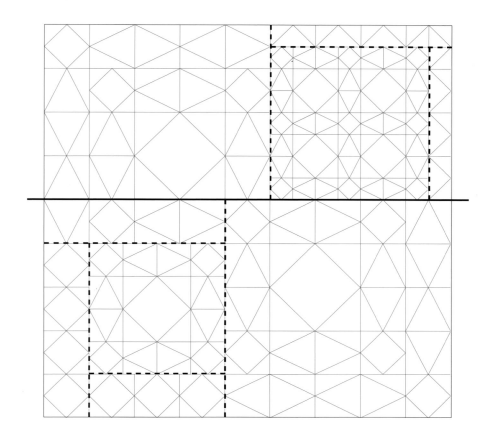

A: - - - - - - - - - -   *stitch small units into larger areas.*

B: ——————   *stitch larger areas together.*

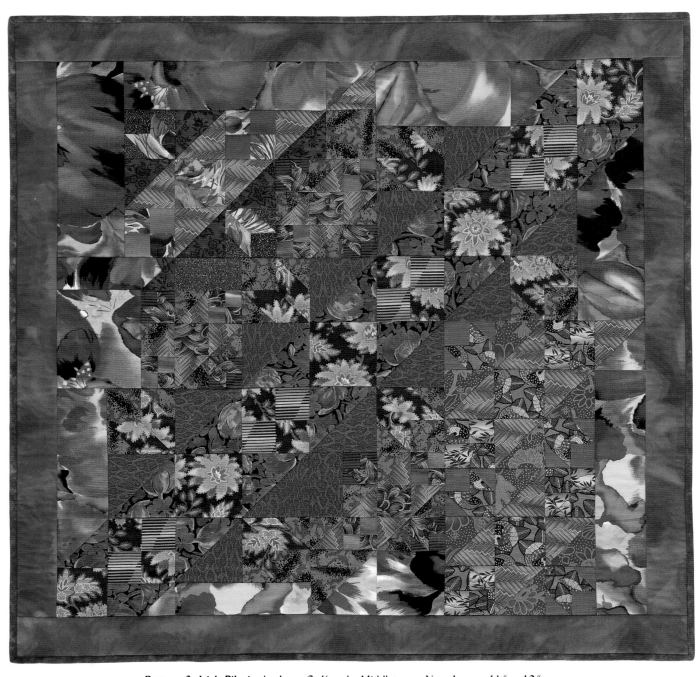

Pattern 6: **Irish Pilgrim** by Lynn G. Kough, Middletown, New Jersey, 41″ x 40″.

Pattern 6: *Lynn's design – Irish Pilgrim (41" x 40")*

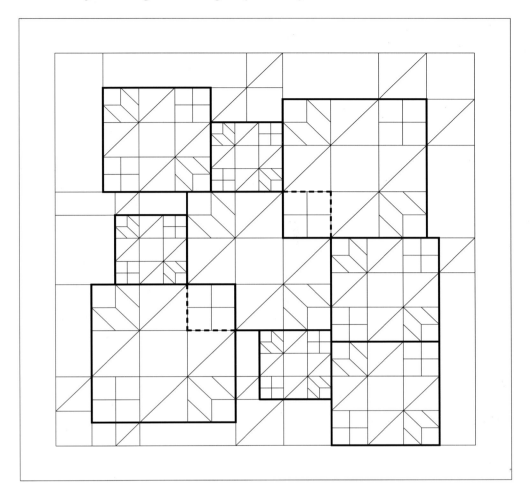

Block: Dublin Steps

Block size: 12", 9", 6"

Split-outs for this design:

Pattern 6 Block

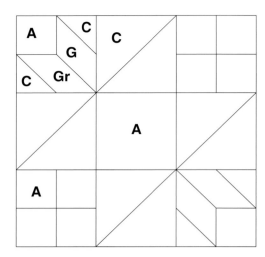

Block Size	Templates
12″	A4, A2 C4, C2 G - Gr4
9″	A3, A1-1/2 C3, C1-1/2 G - Gr3
6″	A2, A1 C2, C1 G - Gr2
Consult the quick-cutting chart on page 148 for A and C if desired.	

Remember:
As block sizes change, the template letter remains constant. Template numbers reflect block size changes.

Templates can be found on pages 149-151.

The "r" designation means a REVERSE template.

Pattern 6 Split-outs

4", 3", 2" finished
A4, A3, A2

4", 3", 2" finished
C4, C3, C2

Pattern 6 Unit Construction

1. Assemble the small units first for this quilt.
2. Consult the construction diagram. Stitch units into blocks or larger areas where indicated.
3. Incorporate partial border pieces and split-outs into the larger areas.
4. Add the outside borders.

Border and split-out measurements (finished)

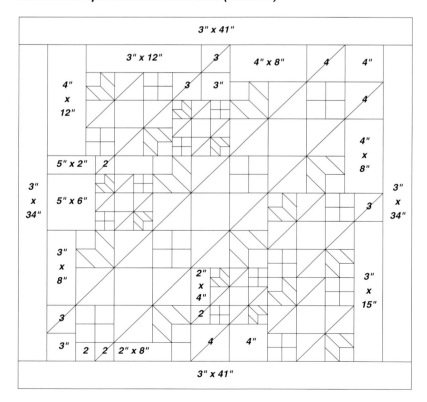

Pattern 6: *Irish Pilgrim*

       Construction areas

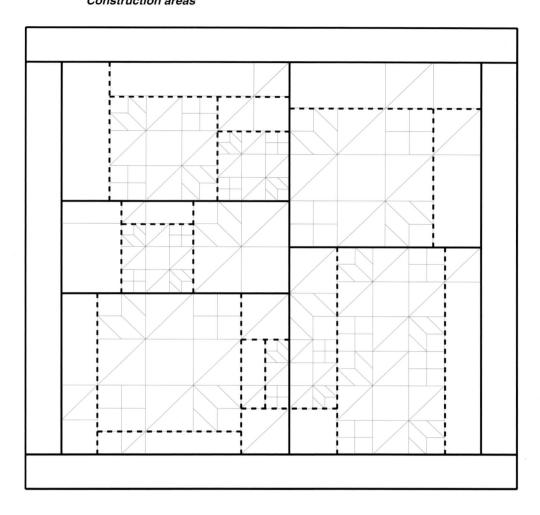

A: - - - - - - - - - - *stitch small units into larger areas.*

B: ——————— *stitch together larger areas.*

C: add outside border.

QUICK-CUTTING CHART

Squares (A templates), half-square triangles (C templates), and quarter-square triangles (D templates) can be quick-cut using your rotary tools, if you so desire. The chart below shows templates and how to rotary cut the equivalent shape.

To cut two half-square triangles equal to the ***C template,*** first cut a square in the size given to the right of the template (1). Then cut that square once on the diagonal (2).

To cut four quarter-square triangles equal to the ***D template,*** first cut a square in the size given to the right of the template (1). Then cut that square twice on the diagonal (2).

		Template	Cut Size	Finished Size	
A		**A4**	**4-1/2"**	**4"**	
		A3	**3-1/2"**	**3"**	
		A2	**2-1/2"**	**2"**	
		A1-1/2	**2"**	**1-1/2"**	
		A1	**1-1/2"**	**1"**	
C		**C5**	**5-7/8"**	**5"**	
		C4	**4-7/8"**	**4"**	**1.**
		C3	**3-7/8"**	**3"**	
		C2-1/2	**3-3/8"**	**2-1/2"**	**2.**
		C2	**2-7/8"**	**2"**	
		C1-1/2	**2-3/8"**	**1-1/2"**	
		C1	**1-7/8"**	**1"**	
D		**D5**	**6-1/4"**	**5"**	**1.**
		D4	**5-1/4"**	**4"**	
		D3	**4-1/4"**	**3"**	**2.**
		D2	**3-1/4"**	**2"**	

TEMPLATES

All templates needed to make Patterns 1-6 are included on the following three pages. **Remember** that the template letter remains constant for each shape; the template number changes according to the size of the shape. Some blocks require two sizes of the same template.

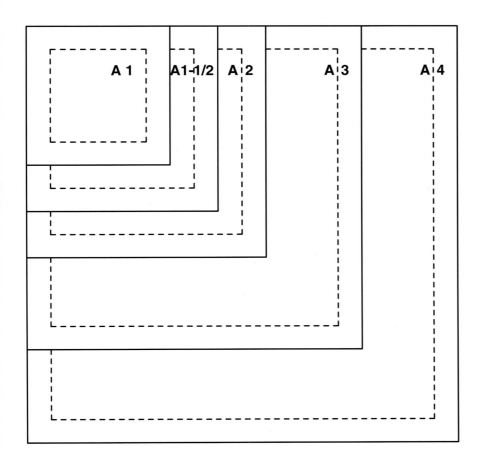

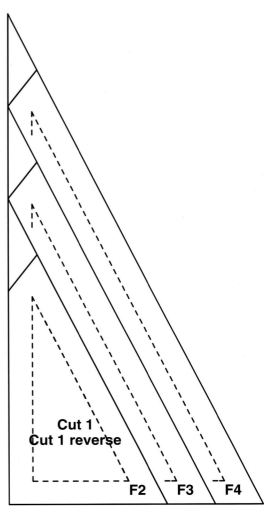

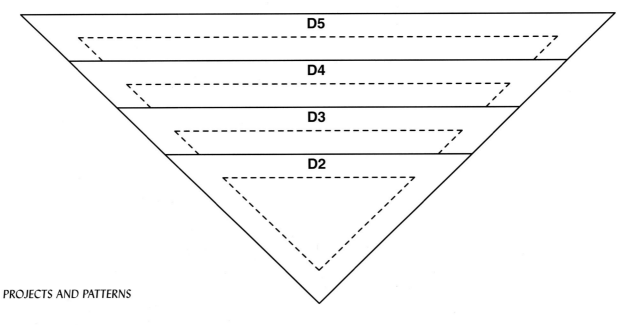

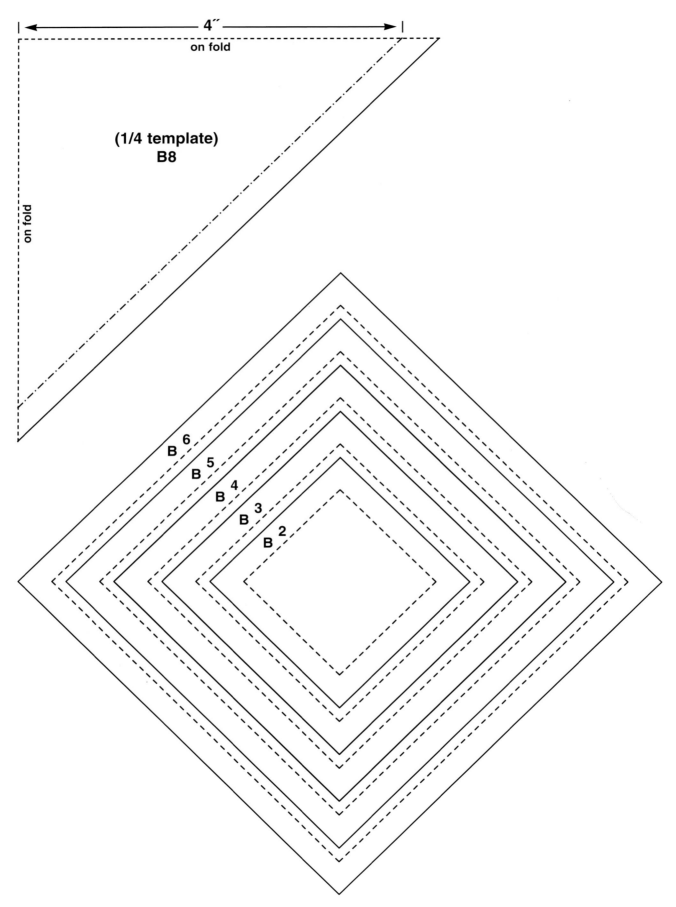

4″

on fold

on fold

(1/4 template)
B8

B 6
B 5
B 4
B 3
B 2

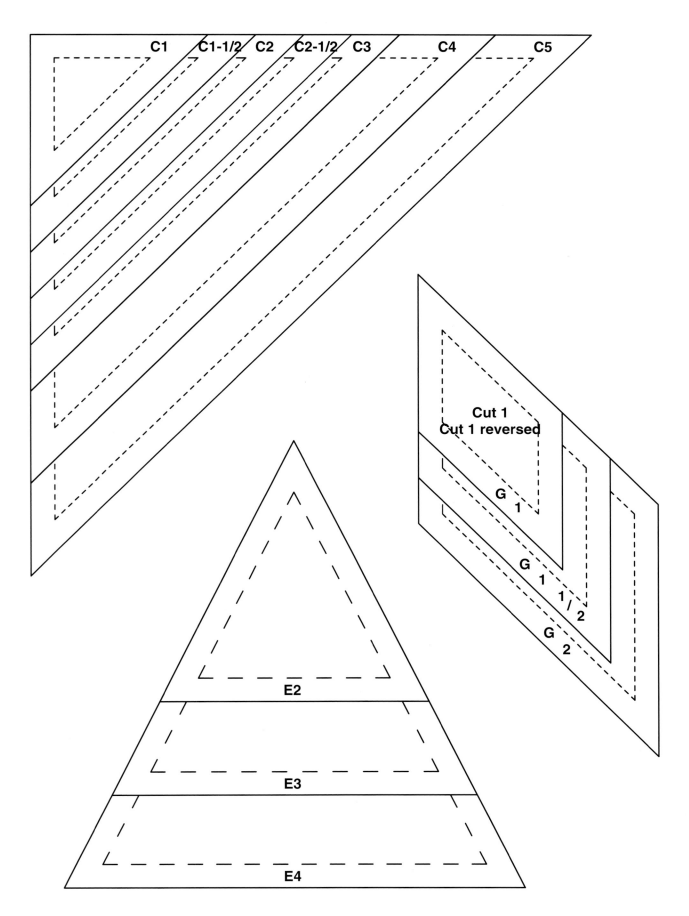

C1   C1-1/2   C2   C2-1/2   C3   C4   C5

Cut 1
Cut 1 reversed

G 1

G 1

1/2

G 2

E2

E3

E4

V Sources and Inspiration

SOURCE APPENDIX

BAUBLES, BANGLES, ETC.
Beadbox, Inc.
10135 E. Via Linda, Ste. C-112
Scottsdale, AZ 85258
(800) 232-3269
Mail order

Bead Source
7130 Reseda Blvd.
Reseda, CA 91335
(818) 708-0972
Mail order

Daytona Braids and Trimmings
251 West 39th Street
New York, NY 10018
(212) 354-1713

Kuma
P.O. Box 25049
Glenville, NY 12325
(518) 384-0110
Mail order

M & J Trimming
1008 Sixth Ave.
New York, NY 10018
(212) 391-9072

St. Theresa Textile Trove, Inc.
1329 Main St.
Cincinnati, OH 45210
(513) 333-0399
owners: Theresa H. Mangat, Becky E. Hancock
Mail order

Tender Buttons
143 E. 62nd St.
New York, NY
(212) 758-7004

"Free Motion Machine Embroidery" and
"Beading by Machine" Video
© Pat Rodgers, 1993
46 Clinton Ave.
Sea Cliff, NY 11579
(516) 676-3342
Mail order

APPLIQUÉ
The Critter Pattern Works
Debora Konchinsky
204 Independence Court
Blandon, PA 19510-9676
Phone & FAX (610) 926-6117
Mail order

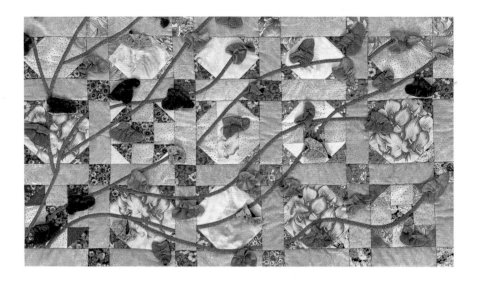

FABRICS

Fabrics to Dye For
10920 Memorial Dr.
Houston, TX 77024
(713) 973-8199
(713) 579-1423
Mail order

G Street Fabrics
12240 Wilkins Ave.
Rockville, MD 20852
(800) 333-9191
Mail order

Lunn Fabrics
357 Santa Fe Dr.
Denver, CO 80223
(303) 623-2710
Mail order

Skydyes
83 Richmond Lane
West Hartford, CT 06117
(203) 232-1429
Mail order

THREADS

Web of Thread
3240 Lone Oak Rd., Suite 124
Paducah, KY 42003
(502) 554-8185
FAX: (502) 554-8257
Mail order

IDEAS...

ART/QUILT Magazine
9543 Meadowbriar
Houston, TX 77063-3812

BEAD and Button Magazine
P.O. Box 56485
Boulder, CO 80322-6485

Ornament Magazine
Ornament Incorporated
P.O. Box 2349
San Marcos, CA 92079-2349

PieceWork Magazine
Interweave Press, Inc.
201 East Fourth Street
Loveland, CO 80537

Threads Magazine
The Taunton Press, Inc.
63 S. Main St.
P.O. Box 5506
Newtown, CT 06470-5506

BIBLIOGRAPHY

Allen, Jeanne. *Designer's Guide to Color 3*. San Francisco: Chronicle Books, 1986.

Beyer, Jinny. *The Quilter's Album of Blocks and Borders*. McLean, VA: EPM Publications, Inc., 1986.

Birren, Faber. *Creative Color*. West Chester, PA: Schiffer Publishing Ltd., 1987.

Birren, Faber. *Principles of Color*. West Chester, PA: Schiffer Publishing Ltd., 1987.

Dietrich, Mimi. *Happy Endings: Finishing the Edges of Your Quilt*. Bothell, WA: That Patchwork Place, 1987.

Ericson, Lois. *Fabrics.....Reconstructed*. Salem, OR: Eric's Press, 1985.

Ericson, Lois. *texture.......a closer look*. Salem, OR: Eric's Press, 1987.

Hargrave, Harriet. *Heirloom Machine Quilting*. Lafayette, CA: C & T Publishing, 1990.

Kobayashi, Shigenobu, ed. *A Book of Colors*. Tokyo and New York: Kodansha International, 1987.

Leland, Nita. *Exploring Color*. Cincinnati: North Light Books, 1985.

Malone, Maggie. *500 Full-Size Patchwork Patterns*. New York: Sterling Publishing Co., Inc., 1985.

Martin, Judy. *Judy Martin's Ultimate Book of Quilt Block Patterns*. Grinnell, IA: Crosley-Griffith Publishing Co., 1988.

Martin, Judy. *Scraps, Blocks and Quilts*. Grinnell, IA: Crosley-Griffith Publishing Co., 1990.

Martin, Nancy J. *Back to Square One*. Bothell, WA: That Patchwork Place, 1988.

McCloskey, Marsha. *Lessons in Machine Piecing.* Bothell, WA: That Patchwork Place, 1990.

McDowell, Ruth B. *Pattern on Pattern.* Gualala, CA: The Quilt Digest Press, 1991.

McKelvey, Susan. *Friendship's Offering — Techniques and Inspiration for Writing on Quilts.* Lafayette, CA: C & T Publishing, 1990.

McKelvey, Susan. *A Treasury of Quilt Labels.* Lafayette, CA: C & T Publishing, 1993.

Morris, Patricia J. *The Ins and Outs: Perfecting the Quilting Stitch.* Paducah, KY: American Quilter's Society, 1990.

Penders, Mary Coyne. *Color and Cloth.* San Francisco: The Quilt Digest Press, 1989.

Porcella, Yvonne. *A Colorful Book.* Modesto, CA: Porcella Studios, 1986.

Roberts, Sharee Dawn. *Creative Machine Art.* Paducah, KY: American Quilter's Society, 1992.

Roukes, Nicholas. *Design Synectics.* Worcester, MA: Davis Publications, Inc., 1988.

Shibukawa, Ikuyoshi and Takahashi, Yumi. *Designer's Guide to Color 4.* San Francisco: Chronicle Books, 1990.

Sienkiewicz, Elly. *Baltimore Beauties and Beyond.* Vol 1. Lafayette, CA: C & T Publishing, 1989.

Wolfrom, Joen. *The Magical Effects of Color.* Lafayette, CA: C & T Publishing, 1992.

Wong, Wucius. *Principles of Color Design.* New York: Van Nostrand Reinhold, 1987.

INDEX TO QUILTS AND QUILTMAKERS

INDEX TO BLOCK PATTERNS

The block patterns used in the illustrations and exercises were taken from four books:

A. Beyer, Jinny. *The Quilter's Album of Blocks and Borders.*

B. Malone, Maggie. *500 Full-Size Patchwork Patterns.*

C. Martin, Judy. *Judy Martin's Ultimate Book of Quilt Block Patterns.*

D. Martin, Judy. *Scraps, Blocks and Quilts.*

VI Teaching Plan

What follows are general guidelines for teaching classes using this design system. Encourage your students to thoroughly understand the basic concepts and then to follow their own instincts. Beginners who are familiar with basic block construction, can be just as successful in building these designs as the more experienced quilter. Constructive student interaction should be emphasized throughout the course. *Note:* It may be helpful to plan a two week interval between lessons 5 and 6.

LESSON 1: THE SYSTEM

In class:
- Introduce and explain the terms sizing, splices, and split-outs.
- Define and illustrate grids.
- Demonstrate criteria for block selection.
- Discuss motivation or theme for these quilts.
- Lead students through Work Stations I (p. 23), II (p. 27), and III (p. 31).

At home:
Students should
a. Read the section, *The Design System* pp. 10-38.
b. Select a block for sizing or splicing.
c. Draw split-outs from this block and determine their sizes.

LESSON 2: DESIGN STRATEGY

In class:
- Review student block selection and quilt themes.
- Discuss visual weight and movement.
- Lead students through Work Stations IV (p. 52), and V (p. 60).
- Discuss border options and construction methods.

At home:
Students should
a. Read the section, *Design Strategy,* pp. 39-73.
b. Draw several quilt designs based on their selected block.
c. Draw several border designs.

LESSON 3: COLOR

In class:
- Review student designs.
- Discuss color both in terms of intuitive selection based on quilt themes and in terms of harmonies based on color wheels.
- Explain and illustrate emphasis areas, using Figures 3.6A-E on pages 82-85.
- Lead students through Work Stations VI (p. 86), and VII (p. 95).

At home:
Students should
a. Read the section, *Color,* pp. 74-98.
b. Discover and draw emphasis areas in their quilt designs.
c. Audition several color selections for their quilts.

LESSON 4: FABRIC I

In class:
- Review student designs with new emphasis area and color selections.
- Discuss fabric selection including types and amounts.
- Show how to make a fabric mock-up.
- Discuss and illustrate quick-cutting of certain shapes and template preparation.

At home:
Students should
a. Read the section, *Fabric,* pp. 99-108.
b. Determine block shapes and sizes. Figure appropriate quick-cutting methods and/or make templates.
c. Select a fabric grouping for the quilt.
d. *(optional)* Make a fabric mock-up.

LESSON 5: FABRIC II

In class:
- Review student block shapes and sizes. Check templates.

- Critique fabric groupings. Note any possible problems.
- Share fabric mock-ups.
- Discuss using the design wall.
- Help students plan construction of their quilt tops.
- Discuss surface design possibilities.

At home:
Students should
a. Read the section, *Surface Ornamentation,* pp. 108-115.
b. Cut fabrics and put them in place on the design wall.
c. When arrangement is complete, stitch the pieces together.
d. Add ornamentation, if appropriate (OR wait until the quilting is completed).

LESSON 6: QUILTING & FINISHING

In class:
- Share the stitched (or at least - pinned!) quilt top.
- Discuss quilting methods and designs.
- Consider marking procedures.
- Discuss batting choices.
- Present ideas for creating backings which complete the quilt theme.
- Remind students to label/document their work.
- Plan a reunion date to exhibit and enjoy the quilts, plus share any additional ones created in response to the class.

At home:
Students should
a. Read the section, *The Other Half,* pp. 116-121.
b. Complete and enjoy the quilt!
c. Attend the reunion.
d. Make another quilt, this time exploring a different aspect of the system... **What if?**

About
The Author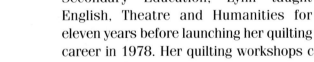

Lynn Kough made her first quilt in 1965, of wool and corduroy scraps, backed by an old army blanket! "Lovely," she laughs. Since that innovative beginning, Lynn has gained recognition for her work with color and design, illustrated by her many award-winning quilts in guild and gallery shows.

Her lively teaching and lecturing style reflects her background in Speech and Theatre. With a Master's degree in Secondary Education, Lynn taught English, Theatre and Humanities for eleven years before launching her quilting career in 1978. Her quilting workshops continue to be received with great enthusiasm throughout the mid-Atlantic region.

Lynn lives in Middletown, New Jersey, with her husband, two daughters, many dogs, an inordinate amount of fabric and thread, and a vacuum cleaner on the verge of cardiac arrest!